To REBECCA

THANK YOU FOR BEING YOUR
WONDERFUL SELF.
WE HOPE THIS BOOK BRINGS
YOU JOY.

YOUR DAILY

All On The Board

COMPANION

LOVE

XX

YOUR DAILY

All On The Board

COMPANION

Inspiring words to take you from morning to night

yellow
kite

INTRODUCTION

Introduction

Hello You. Hope you're doing alright?

If you own our first book: welcome back and thanks so much for buying our second one. Or maybe it was a gift? Well, what a fantastic person that somebody is for buying you such an awesome present (if we do say so ourselves) and they clearly think highly of you. And why shouldn't they? You're flipping great.

If you are new to us: it's so nice to have you here and you're more than welcome.

We won't go into too much detail about our beginnings, because we explained that in our first book, but here's a brief intro for any newbies to us:

We are Ian Redpath and Jeremy Chopra, two customer service assistants working for Transport for London who started writing original poems on station information boards at various Tube stations across London in 2017 for people going to music concerts. We have made newspaper headlines a few times, been on the TV and radio occasionally, and some of our posts went viral a couple of times. We even had celebrities – from Michelle Obama and Katy Perry to Liam Gallagher and the Royal Family – sharing our creations.

We used to wear masks (they looked creepy but they were the cheapest we could find) to remain anonymous and called ourselves N1 (Ian) and E1 (Jeremy), which stands for 'No One' and 'Everyone'.

We stopped being anonymous when we released our first book in 2020, and replaced those creepy masks with surgical ones as a show of solidarity to everyone helping to prevent the spread of Covid.

(Also, those previous masks were becoming very uncomfortable to wear – they would leave indentations in our faces, possibly because they were shrinking or our heads were getting bigger!)

So why did we get started? Well, we both have our health and mental health conditions, from ulcerative colitis and tinnitus to depression and eating disorders. One day we started writing about those and they seemed to resonate with people and made them feel less alone, so we continued. We speak from the heart about what we have been through, and for the conditions we don't have, we research and try to get the boards as accurate as we possibly can. We are not medical health experts, doctors, self-help gurus or motivational speakers. We are two human beings who like getting creative and want the world to be a better, kinder place.

We were blown away by the response to our first book. Every time we walked past a bookshop we would go in just to see our book on the shelves to make sure it wasn't a dream. Occasionally we would take photos of ourselves holding the book as evidence to ourselves that it had actually happened. From the corners of our eyes we could see the bemused looks of sales assistants or bookshop customers possibly thinking, 'Who the blooming heck takes a selfie with a book?'.

We gained over a million lovely followers across our social media platforms and even ended up getting one of those blue ticks that celebrities get. Of course, we are not celebrities at all, and what do we actually do with a blue tick? A blue tick doesn't get us a discount at the local supermarket and doesn't help with washing up the dirty dishes. But it was exciting to have anyway.

The weirdest and nicest thing (we will probably never get used to) is having people recognise us, asking to have photos taken with us or for us to sign a copy of the book.

We absolutely love meeting people and we don't bite, so please do come by to see us; we'll let you know what Tube station we are working at and you can come by for a little get together. (Although, if this book does spectacularly well and sells millions, there's a chance that we may no longer be working for Transport for London in a Tube station; you might find us sunbathing on a private yacht somewhere in the Mediterranean instead, but we will still sort something out where we get to meet up with you and have a cup of tea and all that jazz.)

So, without wanting to sound like we are blowing our own trumpets (mind you, nobody else will blow them), we are just very proud of what we have achieved. Our first book became a *Sunday Times* bestseller on three occasions and it got to number one on Amazon, with thousands of positive reviews, which we were absolutely over the moon about. And now we have been given the chance to do a second book.

And this is it: Ta-Dah!!!

We want this book to be there for you whenever you need it to be. Whatever time of day it is, whatever kind of day it is, whatever season it is, whatever year it is, it's there for you every day, wherever you are in the world and will always be with you for life. This book wants to be your friend and will be your friend.

It won't give you the winning numbers for the lottery or buy you a fancy meal, but it will remind you that however lonely you feel, you are not alone. It will provide you with words that you need to read, however you're feeling. You can turn to it whenever you want to.

In *Your Daily Companion* you'll find lots of brand new boards and we've also included lots of new treats, such as personal stories and reflections on everything from alarm clocks to fears to loneliness, affirmations to take you from morning to night, celebrity collaborations, and much more. You'll also spot a host of watercolour paintings done by us dotted around the book! We have never tried watercolour painting in our lives so we thought (as we do) to give it a go.

We hope you enjoy it and please know how special you are.

Lots of love,

Ian and Jeremy

All On The Board

GOOD
MORNING

Waking up

I genuinely am not a morning person. I'm a night owl, always have been. I definitely have a love of the moon. Don't get me wrong, the sun is awesome and gets all the best headlines and weather reports. Even in cartoons the sun has sunglasses, but I can stare at the moon for hours (in fact, the sun would probably hurt my eyes if I stared at it as long). I even named by daughter Luna after the moon.

I'm also an insomniac, which makes the mornings really tough sometimes because the likelihood is I've just fallen asleep or have been through a marathon of thoughts lying in stasis when, suddenly, it's time to get up.

I know the world mostly functions in the day, but I can't deny that I've got to get up a lot earlier than I would like to and get on with things. It's annoying for sure, and a total motivation dampener having insomnia, but I've found some smashing alarm clocks over the years and All On The Board is the best one, because there's people in the world who need to be motivated to get going just as I need to be and it seems to me that the best way to tackle that issue for us all is for me to wake up.

A Bed Conversation

BED: Good Morning. How are you feeling today?

ME: In all honesty, I don't want to leave you.

BED: Awww, that's so nice of you to say.
I know you've got things to do, but you know I will be waiting here.

ME: Did I snore last night?

BED: You might have done a little, but it wouldn't bother me because I don't have any ears.

ME: You make me feel so comfortable. I can relax like I'm floating down stream.

BED: Well, you make me every morning and when you go to sleep we make a fine dream team.

ME: You are all that mattress to me. You look after me when I don't feel right.

BED: Your horizontal leisure is my pleasure and it's okay. I hope you have a lovely day.
I will see you when you return to me tonight.

DON'T EVER THINK YOU'RE NOT
GOOD ENOUGH
BECAUSE SOMEONE SAYS YOU'RE NOT
GOOD ENOUGH.
THEY ARE NOT GOOD ENOUGH TO SEE
HOW GOOD ENOUGH YOU ARE.

YOU ARE MORE THAN GOOD ENOUGH.

Who Are You?

If you truly look into the mirror and write on a piece of paper,
What words would you use to describe yourself?
Would the description written down be positive or negative
about who you are?
Do you feel in bloom and as fresh as a daisy
Or is the mirror image a reflection of somebody going crazy?
Is your engine revved up and ready to race
Or have you seen better days, like a second-hand car?

When you think of your achievements, do you feel proud?
Would you rather fit in or stand out from the crowd?
Are you a go-getting trendsetter or a follower of trends and fashion?
Are you where you want to be?
Do your eyes really recognise the reflection you see?
Do you feel like a victim
Or consider yourself a victor, living life with a passion?

Are you confident or do you have low self-esteem?
Do you keep the faith or see it as time wasted if you're chasing
a dream?
Do you have insecurities about your appearance,
And if so, what would you change about yourself?
Are you often anxious or can you relax in a comfort zone?
Do you need constant company or prefer being alone?
Are you happy?
And do you take care of your physical and mental health?

WHATEVER TIME OF DAY IT IS,
WHEREVER IN THE WORLD
                    YOU ARE;
WE JUST WANT TO SAY
HELLO TO YOU AND LET YOU
KNOW YOU'RE SPECIAL AND
YOU SHINE LIKE A STAR.
IF YOU'RE READING THIS
            DURING THE DAY,
WE HOPE YOU'RE DOING OKAY;
IF IT'S DURING THE NIGHT,
WE HOPE YOU'RE ALRIGHT;
IF YOU'RE FEELING GOOD
OR FEELING ROUGH,
KEEP BEING YOU BECAUSE
YOU ARE ENOUGH.

MY EYES HAVE BAGS,
MY NOSE IS TOO BIG,
THERE ARE FRECKLES AND SPOTS
ALL OVER MY SKIN;
MY HAIR IS RECEDING,
MY EARS STICK OUT,
MY TEETH ARE CROOKED
AND MY LIPS ARE TOO THIN.
MY FOREHEAD IS WRINKLY,
MY CHIN IS TOO WEAK,
MY BREASTS ARE SMALL
AND MY BACKSIDE IS FLAT;
I'M TOO PALE, I'M TOO DARK,
I HAVE SCARS AND STRETCH MARKS,
MY LEGS ARE SKINNY
AND MY BELLY IS FAT.
MY COMPLEXION LOOKS OLD,
I HAVE FLAB, SCABS AND FOLDS,
MY REFLECTION SHOWS ME
EVERY IMPERFECTION I SEE;
INTRUSIVE THOUGHTS
MAY CAUSE INTERFERENCE,
DON'T JUDGE MY APPEARANCE,
I AM BEAUTIFUL,
BECAUSE I AM ME.

Alarm clocks

The fact that they have the word 'ALARM' in their title sets the alarm bells ringing and shows how horrible they can be. Of course alarms are useful and can save lives – for instance, fire alarms – but do we really need to be alerted to the fact that we are sleeping and it's time to not be sleeping? Yes, they wake us up and all that jazz, but they are an absolute pain sometimes.

I've tried setting my alarm with all different ring tones to make what is sometimes an ordeal somewhat more pleasant. I need to wake up at 5 a.m. today, surely the chimes of 'I do like to be beside the seaside' will soften the blow when it's cold and dark outside? Absolutely not. It's a bit of a wind-up at times.

It would be nice if we could live our lives without alarm clocks and naturally wake up. The world probably wouldn't run as efficiently, but we would certainly be happier and better rested. 'Yeah, you wake up and turn up for work whatever time you like. It will be lovely for you to grace us with your presence whenever you're ready', said no manager ever.

Surely no button in the world has ever been pressed more than a snooze button. Are you a fan of alarm clocks? How would you like to be woken up?

HELLO YOU.
DO YOU LIKE IT WHEN ME AND MY FEATHERY FRIENDS SING SONGS FOR YOU IN THE MORNING? HONESTLY, THEY ARE JUST FOR YOU.
THERE ARE CERTAIN BIRDS THAT FORGET THE WORDS TO SONGS AND WE LIKE TO CALL THEM HUMMINGBIRDS.
ANYWAY, I JUST WANTED TO SAY HAVE A PHEASANT DAY.
YOU DESERVE TO FEEL CHIRPY BECAUSE YOU'RE VERY TWEET.
IF YOU WING IT ENOUGH YOU MIGHT END UP FLYING AND ACHIEVE YOUR GULLS.
DON'T GET YOUR FEATHERS RUFFLED BY ANY MOCKINGBIRDS WHO DRIVE YOU CUCKOO.
KEEP BEAKING YOU BECAUSE YOU'RE IMPECKABLE.

TODAY IS JUST A DAY OF THE WEEK

It doesn't have to be blue,
it doesn't have to be bleak;
You might be out of sorts,
but don't feel like a freak,
You are certainly unique
with your very own coping technique.
A cold day can turn you into an antique
when your bones start to creak,
Every lucky streak you seek
may be playing hide and seek,
What a cheek if your physique
feels past its peak
And tiredness makes you tongue tied when you
try to speak.
You may get that sinking feeling
when the boat you paddle in up the creek
has sprung a leak;
But don't blame it on today,
today is just a day of the week.

It's not today's fault for being today,
what has today ever done to you?
Don't worry, you've got this,
it's just another day to get through.
If you're tired from being strong
and always questioning,
'Why?', 'What?', 'When?' and 'How?'
Just take it easy and one day at a time
and focus on the now.

Things To Do Today (And Every Day)

BREATHE: Very important to do, in fact, absolutely essential. Do the proper breathing too. The breathing that helps you to relax. You will love it.

LOVE YOURSELF: You deserve love. You are with yourself all of the time so give yourself as much love as you can. Treat yourself like you are your best friend, because you should be your own best friend.

KNOW HOW SPECIAL YOU ARE: There are over 7 billion people in this world and there's only one of you. There has never been anyone like you and there will never be another you. When you really think about it you are absolutely amazing. Yes, you are.

BE KIND: It costs absolutely nothing and the feeling can be so rewarding. Imagine how much nicer things would be if everyone treated others like they would want to be treated. Don't forget to be kind to yourself as well.

KNOW THAT YOU ARE NOT ALONE: If you are on your own and feeling lonely, you are never really alone. There are many people in the world who will listen to you and who will adore you. Use social media for the right reasons.

EAT AND DRINK: You are what you eat apparently. Occasionally you may be a banana, but you're truly one in a melon. If you have alphabet spaghetti, you will be eating your words. Breakfast is the most important meal of the day, but it's not as important as you. Keep hydrated as well. If you're 80 per cent water you've got to keep it up.

REST: If your phone needs to be recharged, then so do you. Your phone is smart, but you are far smarter. Check yourself as much as you check your phone.

DO THINGS YOU ENJOY: You only have one life so do what you like doing. Cats would spend each one of their nine lives doing what they enjoy because they are cool like that. So do what you enjoy as long as it's legal, it doesn't hurt anyone and it's within your budget. Have fun. *Disclaimer – cats don't actually have nine lives.

YOU DESERVE

YOU DESERVE TO FEEL WORTHWHILE,

YOU DESERVE TO SMILE,

YOU DESERVE TO TAKE A REST,

YOU DESERVE THE VERY BEST.

YOU DESERVE A STANDING OVATION,

YOU DESERVE APPRECIATION,

YOU DESERVE TO GET BACK WHAT YOU GIVE,

HOWEVER YOU'RE FEELING RIGHT NOW

YOU DESERVE TO FEEL LOVED AND TO LIVE.

THE WORLD IS YOURS TO EXPLORE
WITH THE WIND IN YOUR SAILS,
SOMETIMES ADJUSTMENTS NEED TO BE MADE
TO GET TO WHERE YOU'RE GOING.
OCCASIONALLY THE WIND STOPS BLOWING
AND YOUR BOAT JUST FLOATS AIMLESSLY
UPON THE SEA.
IF YOU FEEL LIKE YOU'RE DRIFTING
THEN IT'S TIME FOR YOU TO START ROWING.
THE TIME YOU STOP TRYING
WILL BE THE TIME THAT YOU FAIL;
YOUR BOAT WILL BE SAFE,
BUT LIFELESS IN A HARBOUR,
WHEN IT LONGS FOR ADVENTURE AND TO SET SAIL.

START WITH YOURSELF TODAY

Be brave, be confident, be proud and be you,
Do what makes you happy,
Take time to take it all in and enjoy the view,
Try doing new things
Instead of being fed up of sticking to what you know;
Ignore negativity,
Because you can't control what others perceive,
Cherish moments that shouldn't be squandered,
Don't overthink when you ponder
Or if you struggle to believe,
When life seems to be going too fast
Take it easy and go slow.
Be honest if you feel worn out
And as if life is dragging you down,
Body language can tell people more than words can ever say;
Our thoughts create feelings
And better thoughts can create better feelings,
If you want to change your life and your world
Then start with yourself today.

 SHOWERS

HAVING A SHOWER
IS REMINISCENT OF BEING WATERED LIKE A FLOWER;
AN INTENDED FOUR-MINUTE HOSE-DOWN
CAN TURN INTO HALF AN HOUR.
UNDERNEATH THEM YOU CAN SIT OR STAND,
SINGING TO YOUR HEARTS CONTENT
SOUNDING LIKE A POP STAR THANKS TO THE BATHROOM ACOUSTICS,
PRETENDING THE SHAMPOO BOTTLE IS A MICROPHONE IN YOUR HAND.
A SHOWER IS LIKE AN INDOOR WATERFALL MASSAGING YOUR MUSCLES,
BUT IF THE HOT WATER GOES COLD IT CAN BE A NASTY SURPRISE,
THEY ARE HANDY IF YOU'RE IN A RUSH AND HAVE SOMEWHERE TO BE;
IT'S A QUESTION THAT HAS BEEN ASKED SINCE SHOWERS WERE INVENTED,
EVEN WILLIAM SHAKESPEARE PROBABLY PONDERED,
'IN A SHOWER, THE QUESTION IS, TO PEE, OR NOT TO PEE?'

Mornings

Mornings can be absolutely beautiful but at other times they can be quite annoying. It would be lovely to wake up every day feeling blessed and with a spring in the step; well-rested, recharged, and ready to take on the world – but that's not always the case. Mornings are tough and most days I struggle up from an insomnia haze and somehow motivate myself out of a slumber I wish would never end. It's not the morning's fault though. A morning just does what mornings do.

If you're in the right mood you hear the songs of the morning birds; if you're not in the right mood you hear the lorries outside collecting the rubbish. If you're in the right mood you can appreciate the beauty of the sunrise; if you're not in the right mood you squint and curse the light of the sun. I definitely do not start by opening the curtains in the way they do in the movies. My eyes don't deserve that shock to the system, thank you. But whatever your mood, it's best to just go with it and own however you're feeling. Don't fight it, just feel it.

As much as I love a beautiful sunrise, they're just far too early for me. The early bird might catch the worm, but if I could remake the universe I'd probably put sunrise at around 10 a.m. But it's all good, those of us who miss the sunrise can still enjoy the sunsets and catch whatever night owls catch.

SELF-DIAGNOSING
AND FINDING FAULTS

SELF-DIAGNOSING AND FINDING FAULTS

MIXED WITH INTRUSIVE THOUGHTS

ARE EXHAUSTING AND NOT VERY FUNNY;

SOMETIMES I'VE NOT EVEN GOT OUT OF BED

AND I'VE ANXIOUSLY FED MY HEAD

WITH WORRIES OF LOSING LOVED ONES, LOSING MY HOME,

NOT BEING GOOD ENOUGH,

LOSING MY JOB AND NOT HAVING ANY MONEY.

THERE'S NO POINT IN OVERTHINKING AND OBSESSING

ABOUT THE WORST THINGS THAT CAN HAPPEN,

IN THE MORNING OR ANY OTHER TIME OF DAY;

EVERY BAD TIME I'VE HAD I'VE ALWAYS GOT THROUGH,

SO, IF THE WORST CASE SCENARIO DOES COME TRUE,

I WILL DEAL WITH IT AND I WILL FIND A WAY.

SCARS

PHYSICAL SCARS ARE VISIBLE REMINDERS THAT WE ARE SURVIVORS,

TELLING STORIES BETTER THAN ANY TATTOOS;

THEY FORM PARTS OF THE MAP TO SHOW

THE JOURNEYS WE HAVE BEEN ON AND HOW FAR WE HAVE

WALKED THROUGH THIS LIFE IN OUR SHOES.

MENTAL SCARS ARE INVISIBLE MEMORIES

OF BATTLES WE HAVE FOUGHT AND MOMENTS OF TRAGEDY,

THEY CAN CAUSE ANXIETY

AND THE WOUNDS TAKE LONGER TO HEAL;

THE PAIN IS HARD TO EXPLAIN

WHEN THE SCARS ARE INSIDE YOUR BRAIN,

IF WE CAN'T SHOW THOSE SCARS WE SHOULD BE ABLE TO

TELL OTHERS HOW WE FEEL.

The wrong side of the bed

Getting out of the wrong side of bed: what's that all about?

It's your bed and you should be able to get out of whatever side of the bed you choose to. Both sides are right and I'm not sure why getting out of the one side of bed would make anybody grumpy. Falling out of bed most certainly would make you a bit grumpy though.

The wrong side of bed isn't really wrong, it's just misunderstood. It doesn't mean to cause harm. The wrong side of bed for you could be the right side of bed for somebody else.

What side of bed did you get out of today?

HELLOO. HOPE YOU'RE
DOO DOOING ALLWIPE? I
LOVE IT WHEN I'M ON A ROLL,
BUT, I HATE BEING RIPPED OFF.
IF I CAN'T BE A ROCK'N'ROLL
STAR, I WILL BE A ROLL MODEL.

YOU ARE POSSIBLY
ANXIOUS, NERVOUS, WORRIED,
UNCERTAIN, SCARED, ANGRY,
FRUSTRATED, ANNOYED, SAD,
CONFUSED, FEELING
HOPELESS AND HELPLESS,
LONELY IN A COMFORT ZONE;
BUT,
YOU ARE DEFINITELY
AMAZING, SPECIAL,
BEAUTIFUL, MORE THAN
ENOUGH AND STRONGER
THAN YOU THINK AND
YOU ARE NOT ALONE.

Breakfast

Apparently breakfast is the most important meal of the day according to scientists, and Tony the Tiger. They are probably right, and who am I to argue with Tony? He's 'gggrrreeeeeaaaaatttttt'. But however important breakfast is, it will never be as important as you. (Special K will never be as special as you either.)

Before you say 'Cheerios' to your home in the morning it's always best to have something to eat to set you up for the day and to avoid having your stomach talking to you and making funny noises. Eat as soon as you can if you've skipped breakfast. Whenever we help somebody who has collapsed on a train or in a station a lot of the time it has been because they haven't eaten.

I have a bit of an allergy to eggs, so if anyone asks me how I like my eggs in the morning I would probably reply 'chocolate'. My favourite breakfast is a bowl of Frosties, although I had a bit of an incident as I choked on some one morning when I saw that Liam Gallagher had shared one of our poems. It even made a headline in a Sunday supplement magazine: I love Liam and I love Frosties. The incident was neither of their faults. What's your favourite breakfast?

PUNCAKES

IF YOU BUTTER ME UP
I TRULY FEEL FLATTERED;
BUT WHEN ANXIETY
CRÊPES SYRUP ON ME
I TOSS AND TURN IN MY SLEEP
AND I FEEL BATTERED.
WHEN MY PROBLEMS ARE STACKED
I DON'T MEAN TO WAFFLE ON
SQUEEZED LIKE A LEMON
AND READY TO FLIP;
WHEN PUSH COMES TO SHROVE
LIFE ISN'T ALWAYS SWEET
AND SPRINKLED WITH SUGAR,
IT CAN BE SAVOURY TOO,
WHEN I FEEL FLAT
I DO APPRECIATE YOU
BEING ROUND, IF THE HAND
ON THE HANDLE OF THE PAN
IS LOSING A GRIP.

UNDERGROUND ONE SMALL STEP

Every journey starts with one small step
and with enough small steps
you will eventually get there,
Every step forward is a victory,
It doesn't matter how big or how small;
If you feel out of your depth,
Take a long deep breath
before you take steps towards where you want to be,
Take your time and try not to worry
if you trip over and fall.
The first move to a brand new life
begins with one small step outside your comfort zone;
Trying to fit in is being a part of somebody else's plan
So be proud to stand out as you follow your own.
Each step may be small and the progress may be hard to see;
But, enough small steps will start and complete every journey
and get you where you need to be.

Birthdays

The more birthdays I have the longer I live so I don't complain about getting older. My back does though, but as much as it's a pain, it won't hold me back. Age is one of those things in life we simply have to accept so we should enjoy the privilege of having another birthday, or any day for that matter.

We all deserve a wonderful birthday and we only get a handful of them, so do what you love with who you love where you love and don't regret a single one.

I also think the best birthday jokes are found on cards for the older generation, so what's not to love about someone making you laugh on your next birthday?

Oh, and of course there's cake. We should all eat more cake and birthdays are reminders of why.

Doing a little extra

I remember an occasion at a Tube station in central London when I saw a young girl of maybe about four years old standing with her parents looking down at an escalator. She was crying because she was absolutely petrified of it. I went over to her to see if I could help. Her father told me that they had adopted the girl after she was orphaned in a war-torn country and she'd had her legs blown off by a land mine. She had prosthetic legs fitted and was determined to use the London Underground, but when she reached the moving stairs, she was overwhelmed by fear. Her father said they were going to leave the station and get a bus instead. This little girl looked absolutely defeated and it was heart-breaking to see. She couldn't speak much English, but the sadness in her eyes said everything.

I asked her parents if I could try something and they said okay. I knelt down to the girl so our heads were level and started singing 'The Wheels on the Bus Go Round and Round'. It made her laugh. When I finished, she asked me to repeat it, and I said that I would, but I sound much better when I'm on an escalator and singing. She clearly wanted to hear it. I held her hand and she stood on the escalator with me as I was belting out 'The Wheels on the Bus' like I was an opera singer. She giggled the whole way down.

When we reached the bottom of the escalator the parents thanked me and as I bent down to say goodbye to the little girl she threw her arms around my neck with a massive smile on her face. She was so happy; it was like she had climbed Mount Everest.

Then I watched them board a train and they disappeared from my life forever.

For me, it was only doing something a little extra, but to a little girl, helping her to conquer the escalator could have meant the absolute world.

Doing something a little extra certainly made an ordinary day an extraordinary day for me, and hopefully that little girl too. It happened in 2002, and it is still one of my favourite memories of working for the London Underground.

A little extra can be anything from talking to someone, paying a compliment, or even just smiling at a stranger. It doesn't take much and can potentially change our lives and other people's for the better.

What little extras can you do in a day?

OFF ON HOLIDAY

Physically I'm in the here and now of reality,
but mentally I'm on a beach or beside a swimming pool;
I try not to pack everything and the kitchen sink,
but I always seem to be an overpacking fool.
I'm looking exactly like my ghastly passport picture
and it's an indication that I needed a trip;
the fear of losing my passport causes me to hold onto it
with the tightest grip.
Before I leave home alone I switch the power off,
triple check the locks and have a slight bout of OCD;
It won't be long until duty free is calling to me.
I wish I could click the heels of my shoes together
and be there in an instant
like Dorothy from The Wizard of Oz;
If you ask me why?, I will just reply,
'Because, because, because, because, because'.
Drinking alcohol in the morning at an airport is quite alright;
a cheeky little calm you down before an outgoing flight.
Any airport can become an assault course wherever you go,
frantically running to the departure gate is pre-holiday cardio.
It would be lovely to have the money to afford to travel in style;
the only choice many have is a seat by a window or on the aisle.
Isn't it sweet, when boarding a plane is complete
and you discover that next to you is an empty seat.
People frequently look outside the window to check on the wings;
once the plane has landed safe and sound the holiday truly begins.

POSITIVE QUOTES

SOMETIMES I'M NOT IN THE MOOD FOR
POSITIVE QUOTES,
SOMETIMES I'M IRRITATED BY AFFIRMATIONS
AND WORDS OF MOTIVATION
GET ON EVERY NERVE;
SOMETIMES I FIND INSPIRATIONAL PHRASES
ANNOYING,
BY TELLING ME THAT I ONLY LIVE ONCE,
KEEP CALM AND CARRY ON WITH LIVING LIFE
I SHOULD BE ENJOYING;
SOMETIMES I CAN'T BE
THE BEST VERSION OF MYSELF
AND I KNOW I WON'T ALWAYS GET
WHAT I DESERVE.
SOMETIMES I DON'T NEED SOCIAL MEDIA
POSTS THAT SAY,
'THE FUTURE IS YOURS' OR 'SEIZE THE DAY';
THERE ARE OFTEN TIMES WHEN I JUST WANT
THE DAY TO LET ME BE.

NO DREAM YOU HAVE IS TOO BIG

SAY 'YES' TO MORE THINGS
YOU WON'T BE ABLE TO DO WHEN YOU'RE OLDER,
TOMORROW COULD PLEASANTLY
TAKE YOU ON A COMPLETELY DIFFERENT PATH;
DO YOUR OWN THING, BUT MAKE SURE YOU ENJOY WHAT
YOU'RE DOING,
EMBRACE WHO YOU ARE,
TRY TO HAVE FUN, SMILE AND LAUGH.
FIND WHAT YOU ENJOY DOING AND FOCUS ON IT,
DON'T DO SOMETHING JUST BECAUSE OTHERS EXPECT YOU
TO DO IT,
IF IT DOESN'T FEEL RIGHT, THEN IT ISN'T RIGHT AT ALL;
THERE WILL BE OBSTACLES, RULES AND FOOLS
WHO WILL ALWAYS TRY TO LAUGH LAST,
ACCEPT WHO YOU ARE,
YOU CAN WRITE YOUR FUTURE
EVEN IF YOU CAN'T REWRITE THE PAST,
NO DREAM YOU HAVE IS TOO BIG
AND NO FOOTPRINT YOU LEAVE IS TOO SMALL.

Mountains

Mountains are there to conquer,
But do it when you're ready
And in your own time;
Instead of being daunted by the heights
that you wish to reach,
Be inspired and admire the mountains
That you want to climb.
The mountain can't be moved;
But if you reach a little higher
each time you climb,
You will know that you have improved.
Getting past obstacles might
take a while;
But the view will be amazing
from the top,
Be proud of yourself
And don't let your head drop,
May all of your achievements
make you believe in
your dreams
and make you smile.

Commuting

The London Underground can be one of the busiest places in the world and yet even when people are surrounded by thousands of other people, still one of the loneliest places too. Everybody on their own journey is focused on where they are going, in their own little worlds of having music in their ears, reading a newspaper, a magazine or a book, playing games, watching TV or having a look on their phones. We tend to avoid one another and if we do accidentally make eye contact with somebody else, it feels quite awkward. Keep eye contact with someone for too long and it either ends up with a bit of an argument or potentially the start of a beautiful thing.

We all get fed up with traffic jams, delays and any disruptions that potentially make us late for wherever we are going. Many of us tend to leave our homes at roughly the same time every day and never take into account the things that could make us late. Bloody trains! Bloody traffic!

It's nice getting a seat on public transport. When it's busy and people are standing it feels like a little win when you manage to get a seat. Obviously if you see someone that may need your seat more than you then it is kind to offer it up, but if you really need that seat (you may have an invisible illness or a condition) then don't feel guilty about keeping it, even if others may give you dirty looks. In many ways, our daily commutes are like our journeys through life in a roundabout sort of way.

TRAVELLING WITH A CONDITION

I'm paranoid I haven't got my medication in my bag
or in the overhead compartment;
I'm praying that I don't have any accidents
in the downstairs department.
I don't want to be in pain, up in the air on a plane,
Stuck in traffic on a motorway
or delayed trying to relax and getting back on track
in the carriage of a train.
I want to cruise, not lose a grip,
May it be plain sailing on every ship;
Insurance offers little reassurance
when every minute and mile is a tough endurance.
I want to be excited, not nervous about missing the flight;
Picturing embarrassing worst-case scenarios,
Thinking and feeling that I'm not quite right.

PERIODS

IT'S HARD TO STAND UP FROM A SEATED POSITION
IF YOU'RE ANXIOUS THERE WILL BE A BLOODY WATERFALL.;
CRYING FOR WHAT SEEMS LIKE SILLY REASONS,
WHEN MOOD SWINGS MAKE YOU EMOTIONAL.
THE FEAR THAT YOU SMELL OF BLOOD, OF BLEEDING THROUGH CLOTHES,
THE FATIGUE, THE PAIN AND THE RUINED UNDERWEAR CAN DRIVE YOU MAD;
IGNORANT COMMENTS CAN BE OFFENSIVE AND ANNOYING,
SO CAN EXTRA TRIPS TO THE BATHROOM TO CHANGE A TAMPON, CUP OR PAD.
BREASTS CAN FEEL SWOLLEN, SO HEAVY AND SORE,
STOMACH CRAMPS CAN LEAVE YOU DOUBLED UP WITH AGONY, IN BED
OR ON THE FLOOR,
THERE CAN BE MUSCLE ACHES, HEADACHES, BACK PAINS, BLOATEDNESS,
NAUSEA AND DIARRHOEA TOO;
PAINS VARY BUT YOU SHOULDN'T SUFFER IN SILENCE,
PERIODS ARE NATURAL, THE REALITY OF HAVING A UTERUS,
THEY SHOULDN'T BE SEEN AS DIRTY OR SINFUL,
A SHAMEFUL SECRET OR A TABOO.
HOT WATER BOTTLES, BATHS AND PAINKILLERS CAN BRING RELIEF,
WHEN THE CRAMPS ARE CAUSING EXCRUCIATING GRIEF.
PERIODS CAN BE EXHAUSTING, MAKING YOU AGITATED, FEELING LIKE A CRANKY,
ICKY MESS;
BLOOD LEAKING OUT IS JUST ONE OF THE MENSTRUAL CYCLE DRAMAS,
WHO CAN BLAME YOU FOR WANTING THE COMFORT OF CHOCOLATE,
A DUVET AND PYJAMAS?
PERIODS ARE TOUGH ENOUGH ANYWAY,
BUT IF THE STIGMA OF THEM IS REMOVED, IT WILL HELP TO LESSEN THE STRESS.

IT'S IMPOSSIBLE
FOR EVERY DAY
TO BE YOUR BIRTHDAY,
IT'S TRUE;
BUT YOU SHOULD
TREAT YOURSELF
LIKE EVERY DAY
IS A YOU DAY,
YOU'RE MARVELLOUS,
SO HAPPY YOU DAY
TO YOU.

School

For some of us our school years are the best, and for others they're the worst, but the one thing that's the same for both is they are years that do not define us.

I didn't have the best time at school for many reasons, notably, the death of my best friend, a lack of any other deep friendships, being bullied and not leaving with the grades that they call 'passing with flying colours'. Getting through it was probably the hardest thing in my life but its lessons of survival have been useful every day since. Sure, I've made use of some of what else I learned at school (okay, not Pythagoras Theorem) but the biggest lesson has been how to refuse to give in.

However bad school is or was for you, it doesn't define you. Your grades don't, the bullying doesn't and what you are told is your path doesn't. Graduating is not the day school lets you leave for good, but the moment you realise you are more than that experience – whether it was a good one or not.

Going Back To Work Or Education

Going back to work, school, college or university
after a rest day, a weekend off or a holiday
can be a pain,
Walking the same route, driving or cycling down
the same roads
or returning to the joy of commuting on a bus
or a train;
The weather can reflect your mood if it
starts to rain,
You reminisce about your pyjamas and start
daydreaming in your brain.
If you've had some time off,
getting ready and dressing can feel strange,
But it's okay,
You're not alone, it's alright to have a moan,
So many people feel the same way;
Sometimes the best thing about going to work
or getting an education
is going home at the end of the day,
At least you're getting closer to another day
of rest and play.

FROM JANUARY TO DECEMBER

PLEASE KNOW HOW SPECIAL YOU ARE
AND DON'T EVER FORGET TO REMEMBER;
TAKE CARE OF YOURSELF,
FROM THE 1st OF JANUARY TO THE 31st OF DECEMBER.
THERE'S NO NEED TO WAIT UNTIL NEW YEAR'S DAY
TO START AGAIN,
DREAM YOUR DREAMS, MAKE YOUR PLANS
AND CONQUER ANY FEAR;
YOU CAN MAKE THE CHANGES YOU WANT TO,
THE CHOICES ARE YOURS TO DO WHAT YOU WANT TO DO,
IT'S UP TO YOU WHAT YOU WANT TO DO WITH THE DAYS
IN YOUR YEAR.
SEASONS ARE LIKE FEELINGS
AND FROM JANUARY TO DECEMBER THEY CHANGE;
YOU MAY FEEL AS FRESH AS THE SPRING OR AS WARM
AS THE SUMMER,
AS COSY AS THE AUTUMN OR AS COLD AS THE WINTER,
WHATEVER TIME OF YEAR IT IS
IF YOU EXPERIENCE FOUR SEASONS IN ONE DAY
IT DOESN'T MAKE YOU STRANGE.

Happy Places

A happy place can be on a beach beside the sea,
It can be planting seeds in a garden or at home with the family;
Memories of happy places and senses can be delightfully heightened
by certain sights, smells and sounds;
Taking doggies for walkies, stroking cats on laps
or cheering on football teams at their home grounds.
Snuggled up in bed, sleeping and dreaming,
Reading a book or in the arms of somebody you love;
Travelling to unravel, painting diamonds and smiling,
or peaceful in a park making shapes from the clouds up above.
Birds tweeting in canopies of trees on a warm summer's day,
Being kissed by a gentle breeze,
Completely relaxed with mother nature and witnessing spectacular views;
In a gym, in a cafe, in a library, at a restaurant, a cinema or a concert,
Creating imaginary worlds in the mind and taking a break from the news.
Escaping from reality sitting on a bench surrounded by serenity and beauty,
On the sofa watching tv with a glass of wine, a cup of coffee or the perfect tea,
In a pub with friends having a laugh, scented candles with bubbles in a bath
or on twisting roads with no traffic, driving a car or riding on a bike;
Listening to heartbeats, listening to waves, listening to music,
Feeling freedom and a sense of well-being,
Dancing like the flames of a log fire,
Restoring your soul, floating upstream or downhill skiing,
Your happy place should bring a contented smile to your face
and be wherever you like.

EVERYTHING YOU NEED TO GET BY

EVERYTHING YOU NEED TO GET BY

IS ALREADY INSIDE YOU,

WHEN IT COMES TO REPAIRING AND BUILDING

YOU HAVE ALL THE TOOLS YOU NEED INSIDE YOUR
PERSONAL BOX;

SOMETIMES YOU MIGHT NEED GUIDANCE OR
INSTRUCTIONS

TO FIND THE ANSWERS AND SOLUTIONS TO HELP
TO FIX OR SOLVE THE PROBLEMS,

YOU HAVE ENDLESS POSSIBILITIES AND THE KEYS
TO OPEN UP ANY LOCKS.

Today there is a list of things to do,
But every to-do list
Should always start and end with you.
As early as it may be
it's never too late
to count your blessings
and be grateful to be alive;
Just like brushing teeth
every morning you should be able to
have a clean slate,
A blank canvas to paint possibilities
or a birthday cake to decorate.
Do your best to forget your regrets
and not anticipate
when a next twist of fate will arrive.

EGG & SPOON RACE

LIFE DOESN'T HAVE TO BE PERFECT
FOR THINGS TO FALL INTO PLACE;
YOU DON'T HAVE TO FAKE A GRIN
TO FIT IN
OR WEAR A BRAVE FACE;
WHEN EVERYONE IS COMPETING IN
THE 100-METRE HURDLES,
TAKE YOUR TIME IN THE EGG AND
SPOON RACE.

THERE'S NOTHING QUITE LIKE
THAT FIRST CUP OF COFFEE
IN THE MORNING,
SOME SIPS OF THE MAGIC STUFF
CAN WAKE YOU UP AND
STOP YOU FROM YAWNING;
A CUP OF COFFEE OR
A WARM MUG CAN FEEL
LIKE A HUG AND LIKE
SUNSHINE TO HOLD,
IT'S THE FUEL FOR SO MANY
AND IT HELPS THE WORLD
TO RUN,
A CAFFEINE FRIEND WILL
NEVER MUG YOU OFF OR
LEAVE YOU COLD.

Calling in sick for work

Most of us have had to do it at some point in our lives, but is it just me who finds that, even though I'm genuinely sick, when I call in I end up speaking with a voice that sounds like I'm from a horror film, or I'm giving a very snotty and overly dramatic acceptance speech at the Oscars? What's that about? I feel under the weather but I also end up feeling underdressed for such an award-winning performance.

It's all good though, health is what matters most and if you are ill you need to rest, and you've got to do what you need to do to get better. When you're back to your best you can get an acting gig at Shakespeare's Globe.

It's not good to go to work when you're ill. You won't enjoy it (and you don't deserve to not enjoy your job) and you could make yourself and others ill. So don't worry about calling in sick, it's the right thing to do.

NOBODY IS BORN WITH OR WITHOUT CONFIDENCE,
WE ARE ALL INFLUENCED BY ENVIRONMENTS
AND OUR LIFE STORIES SO FAR;
EVEN THOSE WHO BELIEVE THEY HAVE NO
CONFIDENCE
ARE CONFIDENT AT DOING SOMETHING,
WE ARE STRONGER
AND SMARTER THAN WE THINK WE ARE.
EXCUSES CAN BE USELESS
AND PREVENT US FROM ATTEMPTING
WHAT WE WANT TO ACHIEVE,
A GOAL IS JUST A WISH IF IT DOESN'T
HAVE A PLAN.
YOU CAN REPLACE THE CON IN CONFIDENCE
WHEN YOU KNOW HOW GREAT YOU ARE
AND WITH CANFIDENCE BELIEVE THAT YOU CAN.

Brand New Blank Page

Every day is a brand new blank page,
It's up to you if you want to wait in the wings or take centre stage,
It's up to you how you act,
It's up to you what you do;
Don't forget to remember
That no one is better than you.
You can dance to a new beat
And sing the song in your heart;
You may not feel fresh,
But yes, every day can be a fresh start.
Look for the good in all situations,
Look for the opportunities in how you can grow;
Look for the lessons that you can be learning
As the world is turning,
Look for the changes you can make in your life
By letting some things go.
Maybe the chapters of your past haven't always gone your way;
Pick up a pen and start writing a future
That will change your history from today.

AS GOOD AS YOU ARE AT BEING YOU

When you're wrapped up in the present
it's hard to see every day as a gift;
When you carry the weight of the world on your shoulders
it's sometimes too heavy to give your spirit a lift.
When it comes to unlocking your full potential
you truly hold the key;
If you lose it don't drive yourself mental,
Be gentle until you find the strength
to break the chains and set yourself free.
Just be you and do what you do,
There's no need to impress anyone else
by being fake with impersonations and imitations;
Instead of being a tribute act,
let people pay tribute to you
and how you get through tough times and situations.
If there are moments when you don't feel good enough
with the way you look, with what you say and what you do;
Please remember that there is nobody on Earth
as good as you are at being you.

IT'S HARD TO ALWAYS PREDICT THE WEATHER,
 THERE'S NO NEED TO PRETEND;
THE ONLY THING THAT'S GUARANTEED
IS THAT EVERY STORM WILL END.
IF IT'S RAINING WHAT'S THE POINT IN COMPLAINING?
THERE'S NOT MUCH WE CAN DO;
SOMETIMES THE DARK CLOUDS FEEL HEAVY
    AND THEY NEED TO CRY TOO.
WHEN THE DAY BREAKS SOME PEOPLE FEEL BROKEN,
    EVEN THE SKY CAN BE BLUE;
LIGHTNING CAN BE FRIGHTENING,
BUT IT WON'T STEAL YOUR THUNDER,
THE STARS ON A CLEAR NIGHT ARE NOT AS BRIGHT AS YOU.
IF YOU'RE FEELING FROSTY YOU MIGHT NOT WANT TO
    COME OUT AND PLAY,
BUT I HOPE YOU SEE THAT EVERY CLOUD HAS A SILVER LINING;
TOGETHER WE CAN GET THROUGH ANY KIND OF WEATHER
        AND JUST LIKE ME, I LOVE TO SEE YOU SHINING.

TRY TO LOOK AT YOUR SITUATION
FROM A DIFFERENT PERSPECTIVE
BY ZOOMING OUT OF THE SCENE SOMEHOW;
WILL WHAT YOU'RE STRESSING ABOUT
AND GETTING YOURSELF IN A MESS FOR
REALLY MATTER MONTHS AND YEARS FROM NOW?
SEE THINGS IN ANOTHER WAY;
YOU ARE NOT A VICTIM, YOU ARE THE VICTOR
AND YOU HAVE SURVIVED YOUR VERY WORST DAY.
THERE'S NO SUCH THING AS PERFECTION,
REJECT REJECTION
AND CHANGE YOUR PERCEPTION,
HOW MANY OF YOUR WORST CASE SCENARIOS
HAVE HONESTLY COME TRUE SO FAR?

THERE ARE MANY DIFFERENT KINDS OF LOVE

WE LOVE LOVE AND LOVE TO LOVE AND BE LOVED,
THERE ARE MANY DIFFERENT KINDS;
OPEN HEARTS CAN BE FILLED WITH LOVE
LIKE A COLD, DARK ROOM ILLUMINATED BY THE WARMTH
OF THE MORNING LIGHT
WHEN YOU OPEN THE CURTAINS OR PULL UP THE BLINDS.
THERE'S NEW LOVE, THERE'S OLD LOVE, THERE'S SAFE LOVE
AND CRAZY LOVE,
THERE'S UNCONDITIONAL, ETERNAL LOVE THAT NEVER ENDS;
THERE IS LOVE THAT COMPLETES YOU IF YOU'RE FEELING
PUZZLED AND DEFEATED,
AND DIFFERENT LOVE YOU SHARE WITH A LOVER, A FAMILY AND FRIENDS.
IN A SEA OF LOVE, TRUE LOVE WILL MAKE YOU SWIM AND
NEVER DROWN YOU,
IF YOU'RE LONELY, LOVE WILL COMFORT AND SURROUND YOU,
PETS WILL LOVE YOU AS MUCH AS YOU LOVE THEM IF YOU ARE KIND;
LOVE FROM A SPECIAL ONE CAN FIX YOU IF YOU'VE COME UNDONE,
IT CAN REPAIR A BROKEN HEART AND, AT THE SAME TIME,
BLOW YOUR MIND.
LOVE CAN MAKE THE SUNRISE ON THE HORIZON SEEM EASY TO REACH,
LOVE CAN BE CARVED IN A TREE, WRITTEN IN STONE OR IN
THE SAND ON A BEACH,
LOVE IS THE REASON BEHIND EVERYTHING WE DO;
IT'S THE ONE TRUE LANGUAGE OF THE UNIVERSE,
A FEELING THAT'S NATURAL AND THAT NO ONE CAN REHEARSE,
HOLD ON TO YOUR KIND OF LOVE IF YOU KNOW IT'S THE ONE FOR YOU.

Love is . . .

Love is a guiding star when you're lost at sea,
In any lockdown love is truly the key;
Love makes you feel at home wherever you may be,
It can be as gentle as a snowflake and yet as strong as a tree.
Love is the best medication for any pain,
It's protection from every storm and an umbrella in the pouring rain;
Love makes us all crazy and at the same time keeps us sane,
It's a feeling no words in the dictionary could ever really explain.
Love is a mesmerising melody and the sweetest sound,
It's a pleasure and a treasure to cherish when found;
Love is a hand to hold and a safety net to save us from
hitting the ground,
It's a prize to keep winning and keeps the world spinning around.

ARTHRITIS

ARTHRITIS IS A CONDITION THAT AFFECTS MILLIONS OF PEOPLE
OF ANY AGE,
THERE ARE DIFFERENT TYPES OF ARTHRITIS AND THE SYMPTOMS
ARE VARIED
WITH JOINT PAINS, TENDERNESS, STIFFNESS, INFLAMATION,
MUSCLE WASTING, WEAKNESS AND RESTRICTED MOVEMENT;
THERE IS NO CURE FOR ARTHRITIS,
BUT DESPITE THE CHRONIC PAIN AND FATIGUE,
THERE ARE TREATMENTS THAT CAN HELP SLOW IT DOWN
AND BRING THE QUALITY OF LIFE SOME IMPROVEMENT.

CARRYING OUT TASKS CAN BE A CHALLENGE,
IT'S IMPORTANT TO LOOK AFTER YOUR JOINTS TO AVOID FURTHER
DAMAGE,
MAKE ADJUSTMENTS FROM KEEPING THINGS WITHIN EASY REACH
TO USING A HAND RAIL WHILE GOING UP AND DOWN STAIRS;
HEALTHY EATING CAN GIVE YOU THE NUTRIENTS YOU NEED,
IF IT'S NOT TOO PAINFUL, EXERCISE CAN BOOST YOUR ENERGY,
INCREASING MUSCLE STRENGTH, REDUCING STIFFNESS
AND IMPROVING MOBILITY,
IT'S IMPORTANT TO REST AND TRY TO REDUCE STRESS
WHEN GOING THROUGH ARTHRITIS FLARES.

LOVE AND SUPPORT TO ANYONE AFFECTED BY ARTHRITIS.

OBSESSIVE COMPULSIVE DISORDER (OCD)

I KNOW MY THOUGHTS ARE IRRATIONAL,
BUT I HAVE TO ACT UPON THEM ALL
AND IT'S A CONSTANT BATTLE.
IT'S NOT JUST ABOUT TIDYING UP,
IT'S TORTUROUS AND I WISH IT WOULD SET ME FREE;
IT'S HELL WHEN I FEEL CONSTANTLY MENTALLY SHATTERED
AND CAN NEVER RELAX AS I OBSESSIVELY CARRY
OUT EVERY RITUAL.
WORRIEDLY WORRYING ABOUT THE CONSEQUENCES IF I DON'T,
THE FEAR OF CONTAMINATION AND DIRT,
THE UNCERTAINTY, THE HORRIBLE INTRUSIVE THOUGHTS,
LOSING CONTROL AND DESPERATELY NEEDING THINGS
TO BE IN ORDER AND SYMMETRICAL.
I FEEL TRAPPED AND MY BRAIN IS HURTING FROM
USELESS SUPERSTITIONS,
BELIEVING THE FATE OF THE WORLD IS MY RESPONSIBILITY
AND IF I DON'T ANSWER THE MENTAL CALL OF DUTY
THEN THE UNIVERSE WILL HAVE IT IN FOR ME,
EVEN THOUGH IT'S IMPOSSIBLE FOR THAT TO BE.
IT'S A REPETITIVE STRUGGLE,
BUT I AM MORE THAN OCD.

MORNING MANTRAS

Choose an affirmation at random,

Repeat it to yourself and it can
help to set a positive tone;

However lonely you may feel, many
people feel the same way too,

So start off by thinking to
yourself, 'I am not alone'.

Keep away from toxic people who try to poison your mind by being unkind. Don't take criticism from people who aren't nice and don't listen to people who you wouldn't go to for advice.

Never think twice about reaching out for help and advice.

Every morning the sunrise said 'Hello' to the little boat stuck on the rocks and gave it hope that it would sail again someday.

Some might be happy, some might be blue, or even manic, but when Monday arrives there's no need to panic.

It's easy to be forgiven for not feeling driven when the routine of life just seems like a prison; if you're doing your best you deserve recognition.

Fear may hold you down underneath its thumb; stick your middle finger up at fear and see it as a challenge to overcome.

In your world you should be right at the centre, this is your life and this is your adventure.

Today you don't need bad karma or any dramas; you just want the comfort of your bed and pyjamas.

There are days when you feel like a half-empty cup, but don't let people treat you like a mug.

It's okay to not always have the answers; it's alright to sometimes be wrong.

Open up your heart like you open the curtains and let the light of hope shine through.

Don't live in the past, don't live in the future; be in the present and live for today.

If every day was Halloween we could all wear masks so our faces couldn't be seen, but we would spend our whole lives being misunderstood.

Worrying is a waste of time that takes up space in your head; why worry about things you can't control, when you can focus on doing things you enjoy instead?

If you're hunting near and far, may 'X' mark the spot where you discover what an absolute treasure you are.

Nobody sees what you go through with your condition, you truly deserve some recognition.

Of course you want to feel good, but you would probably be alright with feeling okay; of course you want to feel alive and to be thriving instead of just existing and surviving day to day.

Your inner critical voice can be negative and violent during moments of silence and leave your ears stinging, but don't let it stop you from appreciating the beauty of nature and the morning birds singing.

It's unrealistic to always wake up as majestic as the sunrise, but every day is truly a blessing, even if in disguise.

Pull your socks up, even if they are odd with a hole in every pair, appreciate where you are instead of sending postcards wishing you were there.

If the week was a Christmas dinner, without a doubt Monday would be a Brussels sprout. They are an acquired taste, but it doesn't mean that you can't enjoy them.

Be honest when you're not feeling strong inside; why try to be brave for somebody else or for your own pride?

If a car doesn't start or it needs a new part it would be taken for a repair; don't let it go unspoken if you're feeling broken, there are people out there who will listen and who genuinely care.

It's okay to be scared, it's natural to have fears, but will what you're worrying about right now really matter in five years?

When you're at your lowest point you discover who you truly are; embrace your flaws and do your best, then you can truly go so far.

Life isn't as simple as ticking boxes and answering yes or no; it's you who decides who you are and how far you will go.

Cracks don't mean that you're broken, they are evidence that you've been trying to hold it together.

You are who you are, so do what you can; trying to be somebody else should never be a part of your plan.

If Monday didn't exist then Tuesday would be the new Monday and that would just be weird. If we carried on like that then there would be no days left at all.

You know you can't always be prepared, but don't let anxiety about uncertainty leave you permanently scared.

What Kind of Day?

Hope you're doing okay,

Whatever the weather and whatever kind of day;

If it's a good one you deserve to enjoy it,

If it's a bad one you'll get through it, and find a way.

Work or school day

Be yourself, do what needs to be done, do what you can do and know that nobody is better than you. Your teacher isn't better than you. Your manager isn't better than you. Don't work to the point where you are exhausted and miserable. Look for the good in all situations and try to have a bit of fun here and there. Never be worried about asking for help.

Day off

Try to enjoy it as much as you can and fill the day with doing things that you enjoy. If there are loved ones you want to see, then see them, if they have the day off too. Be as lazy as you like or as restful as you need to be. Life can be pretty hectic at times, so take it easy. Catch up with sleep or just spend time with your bed if you want – it is your personal island after all. You can even stay in your pyjamas all day if you want.

Birthday

Don't worry about getting older; it's all good. If you have loved ones making a fuss of you and giving you special treatment on your big day, then accept it all. You are special. If you haven't got loved ones and you're not made a fuss of, then make a fuss of yourself. The world became a better place from the day you were born. Spoil yourself with as many treats as you can afford. You deserve good things. If today is your birthday, have a marvellous day you beautiful human being.

Christmas Day

Do you celebrate Christmas? If you spend it with your loved ones, then love them as much as you can or, at the very least, try your best to put up with them. If you spend it on your own, then do all the things that you enjoy doing and that it's possible to do. Watch a film or TV. Listen to music. Read a book. Sing Christmas carols as loudly as you like. Treat yourself to a bit of an online shopping spree if you can afford it. Eat chocolates and nibbles. Play with your toys. Do whatever makes you feel better. If it is Christmas Day today, have a lovely Christmas. If you are not a fan of the Christmas period, we hope it goes quickly for you.

Exam Day

Just do what you can. If it's not meant to be, it's not meant to be so don't punish yourself if you don't succeed. Life isn't just about grades, numbers or letters. They won't decide your fate. You will find another way.

Wedding Day

There is no such thing as perfect. Some things that you have spent ages preparing for won't always go to plan, but don't worry about it: just enjoy the day. You are getting married to someone who is perfect for you. Don't worry about the speeches or the first dance. Everyone at your big day is on your side. Try to soak in every moment, because the day goes fast. If you're getting married today, congratulations and we wish you all the best.

Interview Day

If you smash the interview and do well, then that's brilliant. If you don't do so well, don't beat yourself up inside. Maybe it just wasn't meant to be and in time you will be thankful for not getting it. See it as practice or a lesson learned; it will prepare you better for next time. Just be yourself

and treat it like you're having a conversation with friends (without any swearing or gossiping!).

Day Out

Whatever you are doing today or tonight, wherever you are and most importantly whoever you're with, have a wonderful time. You are flipping marvellous and you deserve to have fun. Don't put yourself under pressure to make things perfect, just try to enjoy yourself. Take a few photos as well. These days and nights that you enjoy will be fond memories in the future.

Sad Day

If you're feeling sad, bad or like the world is driving you mad, we hope you feel better soon. If you're grieving, take as long as you need. There is no wrong or right way to grieve. Cry if you need to, it's okay. If you've had your heart broken, things were not meant to be. You may not feel like it now, but there will be better and brighter days ahead. Don't struggle alone. Talk to someone if you need to. Even if you haven't got family or friends there are people and organisations who will listen to you and help you. Imagine your best friend was feeling down; say the same things to yourself as you would say to them. Treat yourself like your own best friend. Whatever you need to do while you're feeling like this, do it. Take care of yourself. You are special.

Sick Days

You might be ill today and not up for doing anything; that's okay even if it can really wreck your plans. Don't beat yourself up about it. It's not your fault. You can't always seize the day. Sometimes the day seizes you. When you are back to your best, you'll see this day as just one you had to rest through.

Wasted Day

Today is not wasted if you don't accomplish as much as you plan to or feel you need to. We never know what the day ahead is going to be, even when we are motivated to make the most of it. Some days won't live up to your expectations but there will be days ahead that will exceed them.

Given Day

That day you didn't expect to be much, or that day you forgot existed (a surprise bank holiday, or when it's Saturday but you thought it was Sunday). Accept it with open arms and do whatever you want to with it. Don't worry about the science. What matters is you feel like you've gained precious hours and sometimes that's all you need to make the most of a day you otherwise would have lost.

GOOD AFTERNOON

Work

The happiest I've ever been working in my life is when I used to work in a cinema as an usher. I was 23 years old and it was the least amount of money I've ever been paid, but I absolutely loved it. The cinema is one of my happy places so getting to see as many films as I liked, talking passionately about movies and giving recommendations was such a joy. The only downside was that I put on quite a bit of weight because I was always scoffing popcorn, hotdogs, ice cream and sweets. It was free so it seemed rude not to.

It really doesn't matter how much money you're on, just as long as you're happy in your job. When I was a train driver I was experiencing Post -Traumatic Stress Disorder after a girl jumped in front of my train. Every day I got the Monday morning blues, even if it was a Friday or a Saturday. I was having bad anxiety attacks while driving trains with up to 1,000 people on board and I was constantly worried that I was having a heart attack and that I would die while the train was in a tunnel. So many intrusive thoughts and what ifs would plague my mind every day. A few people told me that I would be mad to leave my well-paid job as a train driver, but I value my mental health over money any old day.

I love my job as a customer service assistant on the London Underground. As humans we spend a lot of our lives at work so we might as well try to enjoy our time there, if we can. For me, it's all about the people. I get to chat to lovely people from all over the world.

When I was asked what I wanted to be by my careers advisor in school I'd say I wanted to be a rock star, but then changed it to accountant because they told me to stop being silly (I was genuinely serious). If I could go back in time for that careers advisor to ask me the same question, I would reply 'I want to be happy', and I wouldn't change my answer.

If you're happy in the job that you're doing, then that's an absolute bonus. Of course we work to live, but if your work makes you miserable and affects your mental health, it's time to start looking for another job, even if it isn't as well paid. Are you happy doing what you do?

SAD LADS, BROKEN BLOKES

UNDERGROUND

Sad lads, broken blokes, unhappy chappies
and geezers who need a breather,
Don't feel the pressure to 'Man Up',
It's alright for boys and men to cry;
Talking saves lives,
We are only huMAN and we need to survive,
If we put pride to one side and open up
there's no need for us to unnecessarily die.
Don't be ashamed to MENtion it
if you feel like you can't manage;
Please talk about your feelings
rather than soldiering on by trying to silently cover
the damage.
Brother to brother we can save one another
and you can also save yourself;
All we need to do is to be brave and honest
and talk about our mental health.

JEREMY

Tiredness

Tiredness messes with your day in so many ways and tries to stop you doing the things you love. For some people it's all the time because of sleep issues or other chronic conditions. Days without tiredness are like heaven when you have a condition that affects your energy like that. Just being not tired feels like a superpower.

It's definitely one of the things that I wish I could pop into a bottle and save for whenever I need it. Regardless, it's important to know when tiredness is telling you something about your mental or physical health and when it is, it's important to step back and rest up.

Sometimes tiredness is just a sign of something temporary, but it could be a sign of something deeper. Don't ignore it, rest up and speak to a medical professional if it's going on for too long.

SOME PEOPLE SAY THERE'S PLENTY MORE FISH IN THE SEA,

BUT IN MY GOLDFISH BOWL THERE'S ONLY ONE OF ME.

LIFE GOES SWIMMINGLY WHEN I DON'T SMELL SOMETHING FISHY,

I'M SO FISHTICATED AND IF YOU RATED ME I WOULD BE OFF THE SCALE;

I SOMETIMES FEEL GILLTY FOR FORGETTING, BUT IT'S OKAY,

I KNOW ANY FIN IS POSSIBLE IF I COULD GET TROUT OF HERE RIGHT NOW.

Above The Dark Clouds

Above the dark clouds there is always a blue sky;
Eventually you will see the sunshine again
once those dark clouds float by.
There may be dark clouds above you at the moment,
But they will pass in their own time,
Until that time arrives
find shelter and do what you need to do;
Above those dark clouds
the blue sky, the sun and the stars that twinkle in
space will all be waiting;
There will occasionally be rainbows too.

Anxiety attacks

Anxiety attacks or panic attacks can be one of the worst feelings ever. Unless you have experienced one you can't possibly know how bad they can be.

I've lost count of the amount of panic attacks I've had in my life. I've had panic attacks everywhere from supermarkets to the cinema. Panic attacks have made me take unplanned trips to the hospital and made me bail out on social occasions at the last minute, leaving me feeling very guilty. They are a flipping nuisance and when you're having them you feel like you're dying while trying to escape from a burning building, and as if you're going crazy with legs like jelly, and everybody is staring at you while you're trying to run away from something you can't see and get to somewhere you don't know.

But as time has gone on I've become better at dealing with my panic attacks and have realised that just sitting down and deep breathing, talking to people while I'm having them, or distracting my brain by writing or solving puzzles, really does help.

If you have panic attacks then you may have found your own technique to deal with them, or maybe you haven't yet, but you will. If you're on medication for them that's okay too. Do whatever feels right for you.

Panic attacks are not a sign of weakness, because even the strongest person in the world would struggle having one.

Many people have anxiety attacks while using the London Underground. We are not doctors or medical experts, but Jeremy and I have found that just taking someone to a quiet place, away from the crowd, and talking with them, breathing with them and distracting them generally helps. Breathing in and out of a paper bag (not a plastic bag) also soothes.

Millions and millions of people experience panic attacks all around the world, so we are not alone. As you're reading this, someone somewhere is having one right now. But, you know what, we survive them. Obviously get yourself checked out by a doctor just to make sure there's nothing else going on, but please know that panic attacks can't kill you.

Anxiety Attack

My mind is racing, my feet are pacing, I need to stop and be still;
My heart is on a terror treadmill and my brain is a horror hamster wheel.
I need to quieten down or silence the vicious voice in my head
So I can hear the breeze whisper to me
'Keep the faith' and 'Things will be alright';
I need to untangle the puppet strings attempting to strangle me under their control
And dance freely in the sky like a kite.
My head is screaming when I want it to be dreaming,
It seems like I'm running away, when I just want to casually walk;
I want to be left alone, but, at the same time, I don't want to be on my own,
I need assistance, but my tongue is twisted with resistance when I need to talk.
Weird sensations and sensing feeling threatened
By imaginary danger in everyday situations;
Wanting to escape and avoid crowded places,
Like supermarkets, high streets, train stations and social occasions,
Impending doom seems to loom and tries to convince me there will be a disaster
If I don't get to a safe place as quick as I can,
But I feel so weak and my legs wobble like jelly as I try to run faster.
I want to shout at the horizon that I'm on the edge of breaking down and crying,
Crushed by the rush of it all and the harsh paranoia
Reminding me that strangers' eyes could be prying;
Tongue-tied and on the inside I'm hung up high and dry
With heart palpitations sounding like planets colliding.
I've got problems with my mental health, but I'm not crazy,
I'm exhausted from anxiety, don't see my fatigue as me being lazy;
I'm sorry for my mistakes and what I'm going through,
But I'm not sorry for being me,
As lonely as it feels, I'm not alone in fighting battles that other people can't see.

BE MY OWN TOP PRIORITY

I SPEND TOO MUCH ENERGY WORRYING,
TOO MUCH TIME HURRYING,
I SPEND TOO MUCH MONEY ON THE COST OF LIVING AND
NOT ENOUGH ON RETAIL THERAPY;
I SPEND TOO MUCH OF MY LIFE STRESSING,
OBSESSING, DIGRESSING, COMPARING, DOUBTING MYSELF
AND SECOND GUESSING,
I NEED TO SPEND MORE TIME TAKING CARE OF ME.
IT TAKES MORE THAN POSITIVE THINKING TO STOP NEGATIVE
THOUGHTS, DEPRESSION AND ANXIETY,
I NEED TO FOCUS ON MY FEELINGS WHEN I FEEL DEFEATED
AND DEFLATED;
FROM THE REALISATION OF REAL LIFE TO BEING REPAIRED
BY REST AND RECOVERY,
I SHOULD ALWAYS BE MY OWN TOP PRIORITY
AND REMEMBER THAT I'M HUMAN AND ALL HUMANS GET
TESTED AND FRUSTRATED.
I'M PRICELESS, I AM WORTHWHILE, I SHOULD SMILE AND
VALUE MYSELF;
I'M NOT SELFISH WHEN I NEED TO DO WHAT'S BEST FOR MY
SANITY AND HEALTH.

I SEE THE SEASONS COME AND GO,
I SEE THE SUN, THE RAIN AND SNOW,
I SEE CHILDREN PLAYING GAMES,
I SEE LOVERS CARVING INTO ME
            THE INITIALS OF THEIR NAMES.
I SEE THE DAY AND I SEE THE NIGHT,
I SEE THE BIRDS SINGING BEFORE THEY TAKE FLIGHT;
I SEE THE MOON TAKE CENTRE STAGE
            WHEN THE SUN GOES DOWN,
I SEE THE MAGIC OF NATURE WHEN GREEN LEAVES
            TURN AUTUMN BROWN.
WHEN IT COMES TO LIFE,
THERE'S NOT A LOT I DON'T SEE;
IT'S GREAT TO BE ME,
I LOVE BEING A TREE.

Cool Call Signs

CHARLIE was an ALPHA male and after a WHISKEY or two
would love to TANGO and FOXTROT with his lover,
On the dance floor they were known as the modern-day
ROMEO and JULIET;
At the end of every dance they danced
there would be an ECHO of applause,
Shouts of 'BRAVO' and 'that was OSCAR-worthy' from the
crowd outdoors
were followed by top scores.
But CHARLIE couldn't stand the NOVEMBER rain and how it
got his UNIFORM wet;
They would go to SIERRA Leone to be left alone
And had stayed in every five-star HOTEL in INDIA and
QUEBEC,
Occasionally CHARLIE invited her PAPA, MIKE,
and GOLF they would play;
Along the river by the DELTA they would swelter
watching the movie 'ZULU' using the shade as their shelter,
a KILO of sun cream was a dream
when they both visited LIMA,
CHARLIE was the VICTOR of JULIET's heart
and she never once thought of her YANKEE X RAY.

DEPRESSION AND MANIA

DURING PHASES OF DEPRESSION AND MANIA
I CAN EXPERIENCE MANY DIFFERENT THINGS IN QUICK
SUCCESSION,
FROM FEELING HOPELESS AND SAD
TO BEING HAPPY, ELATED AND OVERJOYED;
ONE MOMENT I FEEL IMPORTANT
AND I'M TALKING AT A SPEED ABOUT GREAT IDEAS AND FULL
OF ENERGY,
THE NEXT MOMENT I'M TIRED AND WORN OUT,
SILENCED BY SELF DOUBT,
FEELING EMPTY, WORTHLESS AND SOUL DESTROYED.

I CAN HAVE SO MUCH TROUBLE WITH SLEEPING,
LOSE INTEREST IN EVERYDAY ACTIVITIES
AND SOMETIMES I DON'T FEEL LIKE EATING,
TRYING SO HARD TO REMEMBER THINGS GETS ME DOWN
AND CONCENTRATING MAKES ME FRUSTRATED;
MY BRAIN IS HERE, THERE AND EVERYWHERE,
I GET PLAGUED WITH FEELINGS OF GUILT AND DESPAIR.
THERE ARE TIMES WHEN INTRUSIVE THOUGHTS DISTURB ME
AND CAUSE ME TO BE IRRITABLE AND DELUSIONAL,
I SOMETIMES MAKE BAD DECISIONS WITH DISASTROUS
CONSEQUENCES
AND I'M FAR TOO EASILY DISTRACTED AND AGITATED.

Do What You Do

Do different socks ever feel odd?
Do angelfish believe in cod?
Do vegetables in a colander feel the strain?
Do practicing locomotives on the right track still
have to train?
Do careless scriptwriters sometimes lose the plot?
Do pimples exercise by running on the spot?
Do worn-out wheels feel flat if they're tired?
Do potatoes shot from cannons get the sack
when they're fired?
Do mountains reward us with beautiful views from
the top for being difficult to climb?
Do grandfather clock makers living in a digital
world go cuckoo
when they feel like they're wasting time?
Do stars feel fine and individually shine when they align?
Do grapes feel sour and crushed
when they get trodden on and turned into wine?
Do thespians feel like the world is their stage?
And after their last performance take a bow as they
face the final curtain?
Do what you do if it feels right and is good for you,
until what you're doing it for isn't certain.

Embarrassed

None of us really like feeling embarrassed, unless we have some kind of fetish for feeling embarrassment, which would be fair enough. But none of us really do.

I have ulcerative colitis and I have had a few near misses in the underpants department. One day, travelling to work on the train during the rush hour and surrounded by many people in the carriage, I was doubled up in pain and I accidentally pooed myself. Oh no! One of my worst nightmares had come true. I always imagined it happening: people would be gathered in a circle around me, pointing at me with disgust and at the same time laughing at my misfortune, but that wasn't the case. I got off at the very next stop, found a public toilet, cleaned myself up and threw away my underpants. I got through it.

Anything embarrassing that happens to us only lasts for a fleeting moment and becomes a story to tell in the future. I've told you about one of my most embarrassing moments just now.

If someone constantly reminds you about an embarrassing moment that you've had and it makes you feel uncomfortable, then it says more about the person reminding you of it than it does about you. Own your embarrassment, make it yours, move on and tell it as a future story if you want to. Everybody has felt embarrassed at some point. When did you last feel embarrassed?

EMBARRASSED

You are not the only person that has ever
been embarrassed,
Try not to care so much about what others think,
In the future you may laugh at that moment and
it will be a story that you tell;
At some point the people who might laugh at you
have felt embarrassment as well.
Don't carry embarrassment as baggage for the rest
of your days,
People have been left red-faced by accidents
and mistakes since the beginning of time;
For a moment the spotlight of shame shines on you
and you want to be swallowed by a hole in the ground,
But in any situation humiliation isn't a crime.
Honestly, what's the worst that can happen?
So what if you stumble, trip over and fall;
People may have a laugh at your expense and
on your behalf,
But as soon as it happens,
It's in the past and means nothing at all.

FEAR OF FLYING

HOW DID YOU GET YOUR FEAR OF FLYING?
IT'S CERTAINLY A FEAR THAT YOU CAN TRY TO UNRAVEL;
AN AIRPLANE IS THE SAFEST FORM OF TRANSPORT
FOR VISITING BEAUTIFUL PLACES AROUND THE WORLD
AND IT'S THE QUICKEST WAY TO TRAVEL.
TURBULENCE IS COMPLETELY NORMAL,
IT'S LIKE BUMPS IN THE ROAD, WAVES ON A BOAT
OR THE WAY THE WIND MIGHT MAKE A BICYCLE SWAY;
IF FLYING WAS REALLY DANGEROUS
DO YOU HONESTLY BELIEVE
THAT PILOTS AND CABIN CREW WOULD GO TO WORK
EVERY DAY?
IN REALITY WHATEVER IT IS YOU FEAR IS SMALL,
BUT IT CASTS A LARGE SHADOW AS YOU'RE FACING
THE WALL.
FEARS MAY SEEM IRRATIONAL TO SOMEBODY ELSE,
BUT TO THE PERSON WITH THE FEAR VERY REAL;
WE NEED TO SHOW EMPATHY AND COMPASSION
TO EACH OTHER
AND NOT DISMISS SOMEBODY'S FEAR AS IF IT ISN'T
A BIG DEAL.

WHAT'S YOUR FEAR?

Forgetting people's names

It can be embarrassing to forget someone's name. You may have worked with them, or met them many times and yet still you forget. It doesn't make them less important, because they are important, obviously. It's just your devious brain playing tricks on you and being a bit devilish.

Jeremy and I work at over 100 train stations on the London Underground and no places and faces are the same, so it can be difficult at times – though it helps when you're in a job where you wear name badges. Even so, on a few occasions somebody has been wearing someone else's name badge because they have lost their own and so when I've had a cheeky sly look at their name badge (while in the middle of a conversation) and then – to show them how great I am at remembering names – as we have parted ways have said, 'Okay. Nice chatting to you. See you later, Doris,' they've replied, 'My name is Dave.' Of course it is. Damn it.

I've had people forget my name too, or they call me somebody else's name even though I've worked with them on many occasions. I've even been too embarrassed to correct them and have let it go on for a while and then they are shocked to find out my name is Ian and not Bob, or something like that. 'I always thought your name was Bob.' 'Why's that then?' 'You look like a Bob.' 'Okay, cheers for that.' 'Why didn't you correct me?' A shrug of the shoulders with a not-too-sure look follows.

 FEELING FRUITY

I'M SO PLEASED WITH WHAT I'VE APRICOT
AND I'M COCONUTS ABOUT YOU,
ORANGE YOU GLAD THAT I LYCHEE SO MUCH,
I PINEAPPLE FOR YOU WHEREVER YOU MANGO,
YOU WILL NEVER BLOW RASPBERRIES AT ME
OR MAKE ME FEEL LIKE A GOOSEBERRY,
IF I FEEL LIKE I'VE PICKED THE SHORTEST STRAWBERRY
AND I'M BLUEBERRY;
I HOPE YOU KNOW HOW GRAPE YOU ARE,
I JUICED WANT YOU TO KNOW THAT YOU'RE A PEACH.
EVEN THOUGH I CAN BE A PLUM
AND YOU'RE SOMETIMES BANANAS,
YOU'RE NOT A LEMON,
YOU'RE ONE IN A MELON
AND WE MAKE A CHERRY FINE PEAR.
I'M SO APPLE THAT YOU'RE LIME
AND I'M GRAPEFRUIT TO BE YOURS;
IF YOU FEEL FRUITY WITH PASSION FRUIT
OR YOU FANCY A DATE.
KUMQUAT MAY, I WILL ALWAYS BE THERE.

First World Problems

Clearing spam, accepting cookies,
Constantly changing or forgetting passwords for online access to money,
Being hungry, but not in the mood for the healthy food in the fridge isn't funny;
Knowing a message has been read, but it's clearly been ignored and ghosted,
Not getting as many likes as expected for the photo that's been posted.
Getting mysterious calls from numbers unknown,
A crack on the screen or a bad signal on the phone;
Dunking a biscuit and losing half of it in tea,
Being cosy in bed, but needing to get up to pee.
A hole in a sock is annoying and so is when it slides off in a shoe,
Patiently standing in line and people try to jump the queue;
Receiving a 'We missed you' card for a half-hearted, failed delivery,
Left on hold listening to mind-numbing music when calling a company.
Stubbing a toe on furniture, a phantom sneeze that goes away,
A misbehaving umbrella in the wind, forgetting something important to say;
A phone that hasn't been charging, your head keeps repeating an annoying song,
Forgetting what you wanted,
Forgetting somebody's name or when coffee shops spell your name wrong.
Unexpected items in bagging areas, losing the TV remote control,
Suffering because of slow WiFi and videos buffering, and running out of toilet roll.
We all have dramas and even if they seem trivial, it's still okay to have a moan,
If you have experienced any first world problems today
You are most certainly not alone.

I Feel

I feel sad, I feel mad, I feel bad for not feeling glad;
I feel like I'm wasting my time chasing dreams or trying to replace what I once had,
I feel like I should be doing more, I feel like I should worry less;
I feel like a hurricane is blowing debris my way and I can't clean up the mess,
I feel like a monster when I'm scaring myself and preparing for ways to cope;
I feel like tough times try to make me lose the grip on any hope,
I feel like a freak when I want to be special and unique;
I feel like every day is a Monday any day of the week.
I feel I need a life hack to get back on track as nervousness is biting my nails,
I feel an urgent need to relieve my bladder and to empty my bowels,
I feel like I'm slurring words and my speech is affected,
I feel like I would melt under pressure if I have to deal with anything unexpected;
I feel like I'm in pain every day and it seems that nobody cares,
I feel paranoid, soul destroyed and punctured by the daggers from people's stares;
I feel like my tongue is twisted and my brain is cross wired,
I feel fatigued, I feel exhausted, I feel knackered, I feel tired.
I feel lonely with misery for company and as if nobody can understand;
I feel like I've cut ties with every saviour and bitten the fingers of every helping hand.
I feel sensitive, I feel negative, I feel like I'm battling the pain,
I feel like the only passenger with a ticket to nowhere on a delayed ghost train;
I feel helpless, I feel hopeless and like I don't know what to do,
I feel like I should know the answers to the questions, but I haven't got a clue.
I feel like I'm overheating and yet fear often leaves me frozen,
I feel like I could win every race and be first place for being the last one chosen,
I feel like I make the sound of a rattlesnake with the amount of medication I take,
I feel exhausted from positive performances I put on when most of them are fake.

I JUST LIE AND REPLY 'I'M DOING FINE'

WHEN YOU ASK ME IF I'M ALRIGHT
OR HOW AM I DOING,
I WILL PROBABLY REPLY WITH
'NOT TOO BAD';
IF YOU ASK ME THE SAME QUESTION A SECOND TIME,
I WILL PROBABLY CONFESS
THAT I'M STRESSED
AND THAT THE WORLD IS DRIVING ME MAD.
IF YOU ASK ME THE REASON FOR ME FEELING LIKE THIS,
THE TRUTH IS I DON'T KNOW WHY I FEEL LOW AND SO SAD;
I HONESTLY AM GRATEFUL FOR THE PEOPLE I HAVE IN MY LIFE,
BUT, AT THE SAME TIME I MISS THE THINGS THAT I ONCE HAD.
I'M NOT TOO BAD,
BUT THE TRUTH IS I FEEL QUITE SAD;
I MUSTN'T GRUMBLE,
BUT THE TRUTH IS I ALWAYS SEEM TO STUMBLE;
I CAN'T COMPLAIN,
BUT THE TRUTH IS MY TEARS WANT TO FALL LIKE THE RAIN;
I'M DOING ALRIGHT,
BUT THE TRUTH IS I'M BATTLING AND EVERY DAY FEELS LIKE A FIGHT.
IT'S HARD TO UNDERSTAND, IT'S EVEN HARDER TO EXPLAIN,
ON THE OUTSIDE I SOMETIMES FAKE A SMILE
AND ALL THE WHILE MY INSIDE IS CRYING WITH EMOTIONAL PAIN.
I DON'T WANT TO BE A BURDEN,
I DON'T WANT IT TO SEEM LIKE I MOAN AND WHINE;
SO RATHER THAN TELL YOU HOW I'M REALLY FEELING WHEN YOU ASK
ME, 'HOW ARE YOU?'
I JUST LIE AND REPLY 'I'M DOING FINE'.

Time

Time is a funny old concept. It seems to go fast when we enjoy doing something and it moves at the speed of a snail when we are doing something we don't enjoy. Time keeps moving forwards and so should we, even if we occasionally take a step backwards. Time is the one thing we all have in common and yet what we do with the time is obviously different.

Our favourite times generally seem to be Home Time, Dinner Time, Lunch Time and Bed Time. We love Good Times too. When you're younger, Bed Time and Bath Time could be a bit of a downer, but when you're older you do grow to appreciate those particular times.

We should always have time and make time for one another. When a time machine is eventually invented (surely it will happen one day), where would you go in it and what would you do?

I'm so tired of feeling nervous and anxious,
I'm so tired of being far too concerned;
I'm so tired of overthinking and imagining the
worst-case scenarios,
I'm so tired of being tired
and feeling like I've just crashed and burned.
I'm so tired of working so hard thinking that it's
all for nothing,
I'm so tired of my lack of sleep and fatigue;
I'm so tired of looking at other people's pictures
thinking 'Why can't I have that?'
I'm so tired of believing that I'm at the bottom
of the league.
I'm so tired of being convinced that I'm the odd one out,
I'm so tired of my appearance looking tired and quite ill;
I'm so tired of trying to feel alive instead of like
I'm just dying,
I know I've got a hill to climb and even though I'm tired
give it time and I most certainly will.

 IF ONLY I COULD

IF ONLY I COULD PUT A BANDAGE
ON THE THINGS WHICH ARE
CAUSING ME DAMAGE;
IF ONLY I COULD USE THE SUPPORT
OF A PLASTER CAST
FOR THE TRAUMAS OF MY PAST;
IF ONLY I COULD TAKE A PILL
TO MAKE MY SCARS HEAL;
IF ONLY I COULD PAPER OVER THE CRACKS
TO COVER THE THINGS
THAT ARE HOLDING ME BACK;
IF ONLY I COULD FILL THE VOID
SO THAT IT MAKES ME FEEL LESS PARANOID;
IF ONLY I COULD FIX THE HOLE
THAT MAKES MY SOUL FEEL FAR FROM WHOLE.

Mixing with people, school, work

I was always an outcast in school, where I didn't fit into any clique or group and no one, even the teachers, knew where to place me. I wasn't a trouble-maker, just a shadow most of the time; I was there but never really seen. Even when I went to university I spent a huge amount of time by myself, talking to very few people, and this was the same at home. It was a lonely time in almost every way, but I got through by being my own best friend and eventually I grew into someone a lot more comfortable with mixing with people.

I am still very much squeezed by social anxiety but if you knew me then and know me now you'd surely see just how far I've come. Mixing with people changes throughout our lives and for me it's very much a rollercoaster, but its peaks and troughs are getting smoother and I'm learning how to let go more because I know I won't fall out if I do.

If you are struggling to mix with others, if this is leaving you in a lonely place, just remember that you will always have yourself and you can be the best friend you could possibly ever need. Treat yourself the way you would like others to be treated, and you will eventually find your way to a better place.

Invisible Illnesses (What Not To Say)

When it comes to talking to somebody with an invisible illness,
It may be difficult to find the right words to say;
A person can never really know what somebody else is going through
and what challenges they face every day.
Saying to someone with an invisible illness 'but you don't look sick'
may be meant as a compliment, but it can mess with the head;
It can sound like disbelief; like they are not as sick
as they say they are,
It's much better to say, 'How are you feeling today?' instead.
Saying 'things could be worse' or 'at least it isn't this or that'
might be intended to show someone the bright side of life,
but it's not bright at all;
Acknowledge someone's struggles and their conditions,
There's no need to minimise their experiences
by making them feel insignificant and invisible.
It's best to leave the medical advice to the professionals rather
than telling them to try certain herbal remedies,
Eat certain foods and take up exercise,
It's so much nicer to ask people what helps to make them feel good;
Unless someone has exactly the same kind of illness as somebody
else, chances are they don't know how they really feel,
It's nice to be empathic, but saying 'I know how you feel'
can make it seem like their condition is misunderstood.
Don't say 'you're so brave' to somebody with an invisible illness,
Although the intentions are good it can sound patronising,
People with invisible illnesses are not superheroes,
They want to be seen as people too;
Sometimes it's best to not say anything and just let people talk,
Then reply with, 'Anytime you need someone to talk to I will be
here to listen to you.'

IT'S BETTER
TO
SLOW DOWN
RATHER THAN
BREAK DOWN.

Interviews and exams

I've never been a good exam, interview or meetings type of person. Through school all I wanted to do was get out of those rooms and go relax with a piece of paper, a pencil and something to draw. Exams in maths and chemistry and anything else that's not my creative outlet simply isn't for me. The only time I've ever enjoyed an exam was when I applied for a job at MI5 and that was just because I was curious what kind of tests potential spies get. Obviously I didn't get the job, but I do occasionally work at Bond Street station now.

Exams and interviews aren't for everyone; if it's hard for you then maybe it's just not your path. Don't give up on who you are and what you excel in just because a system discourages you. Treat yourself like the star you are and shine bright because you are you and you don't need that to be confirmed by others. Believe in yourself and work on what you do and what you are capable of, and you'll find your way to where you deserve to be.

UNDERGROUND

IT'S HARD TO RAISE A SMILE,
WHEN IT SEEMS LIKE PROBLEMS
KEEP RAISING YOUR PILE;
IT'S HARD TO BE CHEERFUL,
WHEN A BARRAGE OF BAD NEWS
GIVES YOU THE BLUES AND
LEAVES YOU FEARFUL;
IT'S HARD TO BE
FILLED WITH POSITIVITY,
WHEN YOU'RE DEALING WITH
DEPRESSION AND ANXIETY;
IT'S HARD TO FEEL HAPPINESS,
WHEN IT SEEMS LIKE
THERE'S NO TIME TO RELAX
AND YOU'RE UNDER STRESS;
A BRAVE FACE MAY HELP TO FAKE
WHAT'S GOING ON WITH
YOUR MENTAL HEALTH;
TELL THE TRUTH
IF YOU'RE STRUGGLING,
THERE'S NO POINT IN LYING
TO OTHERS AND YOURSELF.

JUST BECAUSE

JUST BECAUSE I'M BEING QUIET
YOU SAY I'M NOT MY NORMAL SELF,
IT DOESN'T MEAN
THAT I'M NOT BEING ME;
SOME DAYS MY EMOTIONS WON'T HIDE
AND THEN YOU MAY GET TO WITNESS A SIDE
THAT YOU NORMALLY DON'T GET TO SEE.
JUST BECAUSE THE SUN IS SHINING
IT DOESN'T ALWAYS HELP ME
TO DEAL WITH MY EMOTIONAL PAIN;
SOMETIMES I WISH THE WEATHER WOULD
MATCH MY MOOD
INSTEAD OF THE CLOTHES I WEAR,
THERE ARE SO MANY TIMES I REALLY
WANT IT TO RAIN.

LIFE ISN'T
A WALK IN THE PARK
(BUT A WALK IN THE PARK
CAN MAKE YOU FEEL BETTER)

THE THOUGHTS IN MY BRAIN SOMETIMES SWIRL LIKE A HURRICANE
WHEN I JUST WANT MY MIND TO BE GENTLE AND A BREEZE;
CLOUDS CAN GET DARK AND LIFE ISN'T A WALK IN THE PARK,
BUT A WALK IN THE PARK MAKES ME FEEL BETTER
WHERE I HAVE SPACE TO BREATHE AND I'M SURROUNDED BY TREES.

I WANT TO BE CONNECTED TO THE WORLD AROUND ME,
NOT CONSUMED BY NEGATIVITY AND LETTING ANXIETY DROWN ME,
WHATEVER THE WEATHER I WANT TO SHINE IN THE SUN
                                    AND DANCE IN THE RAIN;
AS I WAIT FOR A STORM TO PASS I WANT TO LAY ON THE GRASS
                            WHEN THE DAY IS MANIC,
I WANT TO PLAY CONKERS AND NOT GO BONKERS,
                        I WANT TO PICNIC AND NOT PANIC,
UNWINDING AND FEELING PEACE OF MIND
                            WITH NO NEED TO COMPLAIN.

I WANT TO SMELL THE SCENT OF A ROSE
AND NOT THE WHIFF OF THINGS GETTING UP MY NOSE.
IF I'M PHYSICALLY SHATTERED, EMOTIONALLY BATTERED
                            AND GOING MENTAL;
WHEN I'M NOT FEELING FINE AND SELF-CONFINED TO A ROOM
STEPPING OUTSIDE TO SEE THE FLOWERS IN BLOOM
                    HELPS TO EASE THE DOOM AND GLOOM,
WHEN IT COMES TO MY WELLBEING, NATURE IS HEALING AND ESSENTIAL.

Love, Love London

There are no real elephants in Elephant and Castle,
Although in Piccadilly and Oxford Circus there is the occasional clown;
Share a cheeky marmalade sandwich or two after seeing a West End
Show in Shaftesbury Avenue with Paddington Bear,
There are wonderful places to eat in Covent Garden and
Leicester Square,
Cruise along the River Thames to witness Tower Bridge open up
and to see that London Bridge isn't falling down.
Sherlock Holmes wound down with some hounds on Baker Street
Pondering 'Why do ABBA want to escape from Waterloo?'
Along the South Bank there's so much to see and do.
At Wimbledon we can eat strawberries, clap aces and question
dodgy faults;
Cheer on football teams from the terraces and indulge in all
kinds of sports.
By design the skyline changes over time and yet the essence never
alters;
Fashions and smiles can dazzle like New Year's Eve fireworks
and the Christmas lights on Regent Street,
When it comes to unique boutiques, King's Road and Camden
are hard to beat,
The King's Cross because he broke his crown trying to get to
platform nine and three quarters.

Friends and family can get together and say 'Hello' to Wembley,
Lovers can meet in Notting Hill and Liverpool Street,
There are amazing buildings that look like gherkins,
shards of glass and walkie talkies
And so many beautiful parks with magnificent trees;
Cats love Catford and dogs love Barking, for obvious reasons,
Big Ben knows that whether there's sun, rain or snow
London still looks glorious in all kinds of seasons,
A place where you can shop until you drop and pop into museums,
music venues and galleries.
Euston knows there's no problem in getting around,
Doing the Lambeth Walk from Greenwich to Buckingham Palace
or using iconic red buses, black cabs and the London Underground,
Streets built on history, nights of magic and mystery,
Delightful daytime sights in the north, east, south and west;
London has a heartbeat and is home to millions who all have a worth,
We are right up there with the greatest cities on Earth,
When the people of London come together, we are quite
simply the best.

It's Not Always Helpful

If you're having a tough time and it feels like you're
dealing with a curse,
It's not always helpful when someone points out
that other people might be having it worse;
This is your story, your trauma, your drama and
your tragedy,
Your feelings, emotions and thoughts are valid
and shouldn't be dismissed by others easily.
The knowledge of others suffering won't always
make you feel lucky
Or better about your problems and pain,
It can sometimes make you feel guilty and apologetic;
All you might want is for somebody to listen
And to help you lessen your burden,
Instead of unintentionally making you feel pathetic.

Technology

We do wish the world would slow down. We don't know why we need to rush all the time. Obviously, if you are in a race at the Olympics you don't want to stroll up and expect a trophy, but everyone everywhere is just getting faster when we could be much happier if we all slowed down.

Technology has its uses – we've used it to make All On The Board what it is today – but when it's used to speed things up in a way that gets us crashing into each other or reduces creativity to a click or a tap, we wonder if we are losing touch with what technology's purpose should be. We've been asked in the past if our poems are made with an app. There's no app that can do what we do and no app that can do what you can do.

Technology can't replace the human spark and the faster we get, the less spark we seem to show, so let's not reduce our magic to the instant results of technology – let's find that space and time we need to be who we are again.

Inappropriate questions

At some point you have been asked a question by somebody that has been a bit inappropriate. The question was probably not meant to offend or upset, but it sometimes does.

'When are you going to have children?' What if the person can't have children or just doesn't what to have children?

'When are you getting married?' What if the person being asked is going through a difficult time in their relationship?

'Have you put on weight?' What if the person is struggling; they know they've put on weight and don't need it pointed out by somebody else?

Here's some more that you may recognise: 'Are you going to give your baby a little brother or sister?' 'Why are you still single?' 'You don't look ill, what's wrong with you?' 'Why did you break up?' 'Have you seen that spot on your face?' 'What are you?' 'How much money do you make?' 'What do you do at home all day?'

We've seen cyber-bullies and trolls ask people online, 'Why haven't you killed yourself yet?' Despicable people and disgusting behaviour.

We've spoken to gay and lesbian friends who have been asked, 'When did you decide to be gay?' or 'Have you ever tried it with a man/woman?'

Imagine if we responded to these questions with 'Have you always asked stupid questions?' or something along those lines. It wouldn't go down too well.

Also, some people say, 'I don't mean to be rude' or 'I don't mean to cause offence' and then follow it with something rude or offensive. If a conversation is meant to get onto topics like that, the conversation will eventually get to those places when people are comfortable enough to talk, but they are questions that don't need to be asked.

Anyway, how are you doing today?

You Can't Please Everybody

You can't please everybody, it's impossible,
And it's inevitable that some people will be disappointed;
There's only one of you and you can't be everywhere at once,
You're not an octopus with a time machine and the ability to
be triple jointed.
Just because you can't always be there it doesn't mean you don't care,
Why should you break your back bending over backwards?
Or be left dizzy by spinning a restaurant's-worth of plates?
Those who love you will love you for who you are;
A good family will support you and true friends will still be your mates.
If you don't like displeasing people it can be hard to say 'no',
So you end up saying 'yes' to every request;
There comes a point when you have to draw the line,
If you're tired of being taken advantage of
Or you're not feeling fine,
People should understand that even you and your kindness need a rest.
It's not selfish to put yourself first when you feel fit to drop
And as if your bubble might burst;
Even though it's illogical for the universe to have it in for you
There may be moments when you believe you're cursed.
Life is certainly uncertain and you're not alone in feeling unrehearsed.
It's fine to be less selfless and to be more selfish,
There are moments when you need to look after yourself;
How can you help someone else if you're feeling run down with fatigue
at the bottom of the league
Trying to manage with your own physical and mental health?

LOSING MONEY

LOSING A WALLET, LOSING A PURSE AND LOSING MONEY
CAN MAKE YOU FEEL LIKE A WALLY WHO'S CURSED AND
IT'S NOT VERY FUNNY;
WAS IT MISPLACED, STOLEN OR DID IT DROP OUT
OF A POCKET?
REPLAYING AND RETRACING STEPS LIKE SHERLOCK HOLMES
ON A MISSION AND IT'S HARD TO STOP IT.
THAT MONEY YOU EARNED COULD HAVE BEEN SPENT
ON BILLS OR SOME CLOTHES;
NOW SOMEONE ELSE IS HAVING FUN SPENDING IT ON
LORD ONLY KNOWS.
BANK CARDS WILL HAVE TO BE CANCELLED AND THE
PROCESS CAN MAKE YOU MAD;
BUT THERE ARE MORE IMPORTANT
THINGS THAT CAN BE LOST
INSTEAD,
MONEY CAN BE REPLACED,
SO DON'T FEEL BAD.

MENTAL HEALTH PROBLEMS DON'T DISCRIMINATE

A FILTERED PHOTO OF PRETTINESS OR PEOPLE POSING IN PARADISE
MAY LOOK LIKE PERFECTION,
BUT NOTHING IS PERFECT, IN REALITY THE FANTASY IS A LIE;
NOT MANY PEOPLE DISPLAY THEIR FAULTS WITH WARTS AND ALL
IF THEY HAVE SOMETHING TO SELL AND WANT SOMEONE TO BUY.
PERFECT ISN'T NORMAL, DON'T LET SOCIAL MEDIA TRY TO FOOL YOU,
UNTIL YOU START WATERING THE SIDE OF THE FENCE YOU'RE ON
THE GRASS WILL ALWAYS LOOK GREENER ON THE OTHER SIDE.
THE ONLY WORTHWHILE COMPARISON IS COMPARING HOW
YOU ARE TODAY COMPARED TO YESTERDAY
AND WORKING OUT IF YOU'RE BETTER THAN BEFORE;
EVERYONE IS DIFFERENT, JUST BE YOURSELF, THERE'S NO NEED TO HIDE.
EVERYBODY HAS THEIR BATTLES WITH STRUGGLES AND TROUBLES,
DON'T LET WHAT SEEMS TO BE A PERFECT LIFE DISGUISE
A SIMPLE TRUTH;
MONEY AND FAME CAN PAPER OVER CRACKS AND HELP TO FILTER
MOMENTS IN TIME, BUT NOBODY ON THIS EARTH IS ANXIETY-PROOF.
IF MONEY AND WEALTH COULD BUY LOVE, HAPPINESS AND HEALTH
NOBODY RICH WOULD EVER FEEL MISERY, GET ANXIOUS,
DIE FROM ILLNESS,
SPLIT UP OR GET DIVORCED, BUT THEY STILL DO;
WHATEVER THE SIZE OF A BANK BALANCE, LIFE IS STILL A CHALLENGE
AND DOESN'T CARE WHO GETS DAMAGED,
PHYSICAL HEALTH AND MENTAL HEALTH PROBLEMS DON'T
DISCRIMINATE BETWEEN CELEBRITIES, ROYALTY OR ME AND YOU.

MORE THAN MENTAL HEALTH

PANIC DISORDERS ARE MORE THAN HAVING PROBLEMS WITH
COPING AND ANXIETY;
BODY DYSMORPHIC DISORDER IS MORE THAN PEOPLE BEING UNHAPPY
WITH THE REFLECTION THEY SEE;
BIPOLAR DISORDER AND BORDERLINE PERSONALITY DISORDER
ARE MORE THAN MOOD SWINGS AND A SPLIT PERSONALITY.
SCHIZOPHRENIA IS MORE THAN INTRUSIVE THOUGHTS AND
BEING DRIVEN MAD;
DEPRESSION IS MORE THAN HAVING A LOW MOOD AND BEING SAD;
BEREAVEMENT IS MORE THAN GRIEVING AND MISSING PEOPLE WE ONCE HAD.
POST-TRAUMATIC STRESS DISORDER IS MORE THAN BEING REMINDED OF
TRAUMATIC EVENTS THAT ONCE TOOK PLACE;
SEASONAL AFFECTIVE DISORDER IS MORE THAN CRAVING THE SUN
ON YOUR FACE;
OBSESSIVE COMPULSIVE DISORDER IS MORE THAN TIDYING UP AND
CONSTANTLY CHECKING DOORS ARE LOCKED, JUST IN CASE.
HOARDING IS MORE THAN SOMEBODY NOT WANTING TO LET GO OF STUFF;
LOW SELF-ESTEEM IS MORE THAN A LACK OF CONFIDENCE AND NOT
FEELING GOOD ENOUGH;
STRESS IS MORE THAN BECOMING A MESS WHEN LIFE DECIDES
TO GET TOUGH.
EATING DISORDERS ARE MORE THAN EATING TOO LITTLE OR
EATING TOO MUCH;
LONELINESS IS MORE THAN BEING ALONE AND FEELING OUT OF TOUCH;
ADDICTION IS MORE THAN HOLDING ONTO BAD HABITS WITH A TIGHT CLUTCH.
MENTAL HEALTH PROBLEMS DESERVE AWARENESS,
COMPASSION AND RECOGNITION;
AS YOU ARE MUCH, MUCH MORE THAN A LABEL, DIAGNOSIS OR CONDITION.

MY INVISIBLE ENEMY
(WELL, WELL, WELL)

WELL, WELL, WELL,
LOOK WHO'S BACK AGAIN,
YOU COME AND GO, IN AND OUT OF MY DAY;
I WAS FEELING JUST FINE,
UNTIL YOU DROPPED ME A LINE
AND POPPED INTO MY MIND,
IF I HAD ONE WISH I WOULD WISH YOU AWAY.
ONE MINUTE I'M DOING ALRIGHT,
AND THEN I'M FROZEN BY FRIGHT, FIGHT OR FLIGHT,
THE FLASHBACKS ALWAYS MAKE ME UPSET;
WHEN WILL THEY EVER END?
I SPEND MORE TIME WITH MY INVISIBLE ENEMY THAN I DO
WITH MY BEST FRIEND,
IT PLAYS WITH MY HEART AND POINTS OUT EVERY SINGLE
REGRET.
THUD, THUD, THUD GOES MY PULSE,
I LOSE MY BREATH AND I'M FILLED WITH DREAD;
ALL I HOPE IS THAT I WILL COPE
EVERY TIME MY INVISIBLE ENEMY SHOWS UP
AND APPEARS WITH ITS UGLY HEAD.

Why The Long Face?

It's long because I was born with it,
It's long because I'm tired;
It's long because it's too hot outside,
It's long because I was fired.
It's long because a loved one just passed away,
It's long because it's a bad photograph;
It's long because my life's a joke that I just don't get,
It's long because I feel unable to smile or laugh.
It's long because you asked me why my face is long,
It's long because people assume and consume too much;
It's long because I'm not in the mood for people being rude,
It's long because I miss a lover's tender touch.
It's long because I played Russian roulette and lost a bet,
It's long because I've got a lot on my chest;
It's long because today has been tough and I didn't feel strong enough,
It's long because my muscles need to rest.
It's long because I'm disappointed with my life,
It's long because I used to suffer as a kid;
It's long because I'm battling a battle that nobody can see,
It's long because the 'cheer up', it might never happen' already did.
It's long because my mind plays tricks on me,
It's long because I'm going through a separation or divorce;
It's long because I've failed and missed the boat that just set sail,
It's long because... I just might be a horse.

Nobody's Fool

At times I'm shy, but there's no reason why,
That I shouldn't be able to look somebody
straight in the eye;
I may not earn as much money as some other people,
But as far as I can see,
Someone having 'manager' or 'executive' in their job title
doesn't make them a better person than me.
The best promotion and greatest achievement
I can hope to accomplish
Is to become a better person as I age;
Is stepping on someone to get further up a ladder
any way to live
just to add more money to a monthly wage?
There's no reason for me to feel nervous talking
to people, face to face or on a telephone call;
I matter and my opinions are valid,
No question I ask or answer I give is stupid,
I am a somebody and I won't be nobody's fool.

WHEN THE SKY OPENS UP

OUR TEARS CAN BE DISGUISED BY THE RAIN;

WE CAN USE A FALSE SMILE

TO MASK OUR SADNESS AND PAIN;

BUT WE SHOULDN'T HIDE OUR FEELINGS INSIDE

OR BE EMBARRASSED OF SORROW;

LIKE THE SKY ABOVE,

LET'S OPEN UP WITH EACH OTHER

BY BUILDING BRIDGES

AND A BETTER TOMORROW.

YOUTH
MENTAL HEALTH

CHILDREN AND YOUNG PEOPLE CAN GET SAD AND DEPRESSED,
THE PRESSURES OF GROWING UP,
GETTING GOOD SCHOOL GRADES AND CHOOSING CAREERS
CAN BE OVERWHELMING AND MAKE THEM FEEL STRESSED;
EVEN THOUGH PHYSICALLY SOME HAVE MORE ENERGY,
THEY STILL NEED TO REST,
UNREALISTIC EXPECTATIONS, THE STATE OF THE WORLD
AND LIFE SITUATIONS CAN BE TOO MUCH
FOR THEM TO MENTALLY DIGEST.
SOCIAL MEDIA AND COMPARING
CAN SOMETIMES MAKE THEM FEEL BULLIED AND INADEQUATE
AND LIKE THEY ARE LOSING AN UNFAIR CONTEST,
THE MENTAL HEALTH ISSUES OF CHILDREN AND YOUNG PEOPLE
SERIOUSLY NEEDS TO BE ADDRESSED;
IF YOU ARE A YOUNG PERSON AND READING THIS,
PLEASE KNOW THAT YOU MATTER
AND IT'S FOR THE BEST,
TO SHARE WHATEVER YOU'RE GOING THROUGH BY TALKING
AND GETTING YOUR THOUGHTS, FEELINGS, EMOTIONS AND FEARS
FROM OFF YOUR CHEST.

FROM THE STARS UP IN SPACE,

TO THE WATER ON EARTH,

YOU HAVE PURPOSE,

YOU ARE ESSENTIAL,

PLEASE KNOW HOW MUCH YOU ARE WORTH.

When You Need To Explain Your Pain

Whenever you need to explain your pain
it seems like a thankless task;
Reasonable adjustments are not too much to ask
as you try your best to carry on and hide your sadness, the struggles
and the stress
behind a brave face and a happy mask.
You can't show your bruises, broken bones or scars
and you don't wear a plaster cast;
There seems to be no cure or recovery date, it could be a lifelong thing
so it's not possible for you to know how long it will last.
The support of broken bones are visible
and can be easier to fix
than a broken mind, a broken spirit and a broken heart;
When somebody says
'You're too this and too that to have that' or 'you don't look ill',
But you feel broken inside,
The frustration and isolation can leave you falling apart.
When a condition isn't visible to others
It can be a silent, deafening cry for help,
Wanting to scream your lungs out from the pain,
But it just comes out as a yelp;
If you had a broken limb you would get some sympathy
and you could get the plaster cast signed,
But it's impossible to show off wounds, scars and evidence of pain
when they are underneath your skin and in your mind.

I THINK I WORRY
TOO MUCH,
WITHOUT A DOUBT,
WHEN I'M NOT WORRIED
I SEEM TO WORRY
THAT I'VE GOT NOTHING
TO WORRY ABOUT;
I WOULD LOVE TO BE
A WARRIOR,
BUT, I'M A WORRIER INSTEAD,
I WORRY WHEN I WAKE UP
AND I'M WORN OUT FROM
WORRYING WHEN I
GO TO BED.

A smile doesn't always mean that you're happy,
A smile can mean you're being defiantly strong;
A smile can break down a barrier between two people
more effectively than words,
It can be the melody and the harmony for a heavy
heart's song.
Peace begins with a smile,
It's the universal language of kindness,
Smiles can boost the mood and they are also
free therapy;
Smile with the mouth, smile with the eyes,
If the world is dark let a smile be the sunrise,
Surrounded by locks
A smile can open any box and be the key.

Whatever The Weather

It's not your fault if a faulty weather report leaves you short
and catches you out,
It's hard to snow who to gust when you feel frost and full of drought;
It doesn't take a tornado to knock you down or a twister to
get you in a twist,
If your mind is busy in a blizzard thinking of every opportunity
that you mist.
Some days you can be on cloud nine with your head in the clouds

and other days there's a fog in your brain;
When lightning strikes it can be shocking and frightening
and a downpour of tears can cause a puddle or a flood,
But rainbows can't be made without the sun and the rain.
If you're feeling under the weather it's snow laughing matter,
A cold front and back with cold feet and cold shoulders
can leave you cold in iceolation and make you freeze;
Icy blasts from an overcast past can knock the wind out of you

As snowflakes settle on your mistakes
and you wonder hail long the storm will last,
A hurricane causes pain and devastation
While you wish life could be a breeze.
Whatever the weather, let's be positive and try not to complain;
Smile at the sun, whistle with the wind, play in the snow,
sing and dance in the rain.

SMARTPHONE

HAND ON HEART I DON'T FEEL SO SMART
WITH A SMARTPHONE IN MY HAND;
EVERY FEW MINUTES I KEEP CHECKING IT,
I'M SURE OTHER PEOPLE UNDERSTAND.
IF I LOOKED AT MY REFLECTION AS OFTEN AS I LOOK
AT MESSAGES AND MEMES
I WOULD BE LABELLED AS VAIN;
ACCEPTING COOKIES LEFT, RIGHT AND CENTRE,
SORTING OUT SPAM
AND CONSTANTLY CLEARING MY INBOX,
WHILE SITTING ON THE TOILET
OR ON THE SEAT OF A TRAIN.
TEXTING CAN BE PREDICTIVE,
SEARCHING ONLINE MAY SEND YOU DOWN A RABBIT HOLE
AND IS OFTEN ADDICTIVE,
BUT I NEED TO BREAK FREE FROM TECHNOLOGY
THROUGHOUT THE DAY;
I WANT TO SPEND SOME TIME
WITHOUT REPLYING TO EMAILS,
TAKING SELFIES, POSTING PHOTOS
OR THE LATEST STATUS UPDATE OF MY MIND,
I WANT TO SWITCH OFF FOR A WHILE AND SMILE
AS I PUT MY SMARTPHONE AWAY.

Queuing

It feels like a lifetime that I've been queuing;
I've got things to do, I'm starting to stew,
What is the person at the front of the
queue doing?
Can't they employ more staff,
open more counters and tills?
Standing in this line doesn't make me feel
like dancing; it's making me want to run
for the hills.
I bet the person at the front is not in a rush
and they are telling their life story;
as I feel my time is slipping away
I'm not feeling hunky-dory.
It's out of my control,
I know I need to be patient,
And I will get there in the end;
When I'm in a queue I can replace my
seething with deep breathing
rather than letting the queue drive me
around the bend.

PUBLIC SPEAKING

WHAT'S THE WORST THAT CAN HAPPEN WHEN IT
COMES TO PUBLIC SPEAKING?
IS IT BEING HUMILIATED AND RIDICULED?
OR ACCUSED OF ATTENTION SEEKING?
SO WHAT IF YOU FLUFF YOUR LINES
OR FORGET THE WORDS,
SO DO FAMOUS SINGERS TOO;
JUST WRITE DOWN LINES ON A PIECE OF PAPER
AND USE THEM LIKE TV PRESENTERS USE AN AUTOCUE.
BUT WHAT IF YOU FREEZE?
AND WHAT IF THEY JUDGE?
SO WHAT, WHO REALLY GIVES A FUDGE?
YOU GOT UP AND YOU SHOULD BE PROUD;
IF YOU FIND IT HELPFUL AND YOU'RE IN THE MOOD
THEN PICTURE THE AUDIENCE IN THE NUDE,
DON'T SEE A SEA OF FACES AS THE ENEMY,
THEY ARE JUST FACES IN A CROWD.

PRICELESS MOTHERLY ADVICE

DON'T LEAVE HOME WITHOUT GOOD UNDERWEAR ON IN CASE YOU GET
INVOLVED IN AN ACCIDENT,
DON'T RUN AFTER ANYBODY BECAUSE, JUST LIKE BUSES,
THERE WILL ALWAYS BE ANOTHER ONE COMING ALONG;
WHEN IT COMES TO ADVICE MUMS ALWAYS KNOW BEST
AND NINE TIMES OUT OF TEN, MUMS ARE NEVER WRONG.
IF YOU PULL A FACE AND THE WIND CHANGES YOUR FACE WILL STAY LIKE THAT,
DON'T PLAY WITH YOUR BELLY BUTTON, IT MIGHT COME UNDONE;
TAKE YOUR COAT OFF INDOORS BECAUSE YOU WON'T FEEL THE BENEFIT WHEN
YOU GO OUTSIDE,
ALWAYS WEAR FACTOR 50 AND COVER UP YOUR SHOULDERS IN THE SUN.
DON'T BUY CHEAP, YOU WILL END UP PAYING TWICE,
DON'T SIT TOO CLOSE TO THE TELEVISION OR YOU WILL GET SQUARE EYES,
DON'T SWALLOW APPLE PIPS BECAUSE A TREE MIGHT GROW FROM
OUT OF YOUR HEAD;
DON'T SWALLOW CHEWING GUM, DON'T EAT YELLOW SNOW,
EVEN THOUGH MONEY DOESN'T GROW ON TREES SPEND IT ON NICE
TOILET ROLL,
LOOK AT THE DESSERT MENU FIRST, SO YOU KNOW HOW MUCH ROOM TO LEAVE,
DON'T OVERTHINK, JUST KICK OFF YOUR SHOES AND DANCE INSTEAD.
PEOPLE ARE STILL A MOTHER'S KIDS WHETHER THEY ARE TWO OR 102;
SO RESPECT YOURSELF AND OTHERS, REMEMBER YOUR P'S AND Q'S,
MIND YOUR MANNERS IN WHAT YOU SAY AND DO.

GRIEF HURTS SO MUCH
BECAUSE I MISS YOU SO MUCH,
I WOULDN'T AND COULDN'T
LOVE YOU ANY LESS
AND THAT'S WHY
I'M IN SUCH EMOTIONAL PAIN;
BUT I WILL CARRY ON
AND SOMEHOW GET THROUGH
JUST LIKE YOU WOULD WANT ME TO
AS A WAY OF HONOURING YOU,
I PROMISE I WILL
NEVER FORGET YOU
AND ONE DAY I WILL
FIND MY SMILE AGAIN.

OUT OF THE SHADE

WHAT SEEMS LIKE SILLY STUFF AND NAME CALLING
CAN CAUSE SOMEBODY ANXIETY AND PSYCHOLOGICAL DAMAGE,
GROWING UP WITH ISSUES ABOUT APPEARANCES AND EMOTIONALLY STRUGGLING
                                             TO MANAGE,

EXPERIENCES OF BEING BULLIED OR BEING LEFT OUT CAN MAKE THE VICTIM
OF BULLYING WANT TO RETREAT AND HIDE IN THE SHADE;
IT MAY SEEM FUNNY AND NOT TOO BAD FOR THOSE NOT ON THE RECEIVING END,
BUT IF YOU JUST GO ALONG WITH IT AND NOT TELL ANYONE
IN TIME IT CAN FEEL LIKE ONE OF THE WORST DECISIONS YOU EVER MADE.

WHATEVER SITUATION YOU'RE IN, WHENEVER YOU DO SOMETHING,
MAKE SURE IT'S YOUR OWN DECISION AND YOU ARE DOING IT
BECAUSE YOU LOVE IT AND BECAUSE YOU WANT TO;
DON'T PUT CLOTHES ON IN THE MORNING AND THINK,
'WILL THAT PERSON LIKE THIS OUTFIT?' OR 'WILL THEY LOOK AT ME THAT WAY?'
THERE'S NO NEED TO DRESS TO IMPRESS ANYONE,
IT'S YOUR LIFE AND YOU SHOULD DO IT FOR YOU.

AS HARD AS IT IS SOMETIMES, SOMEONE HAS TO PUT SOMETHING INTO
                                             PERSPECTIVE,
ALTHOUGH WHEN IT'S HAPPENING TO YOU AT THE TIME IT TAKES OVER
                                             EVERYTHING,
INVADING YOUR DREAMS, DISTURBING YOUR SLEEP AND RUINING YOUR DAY;
IF I COULD TELL SOMETHING TO MYSELF BACK THEN,
IT WOULD BE THIS DOESN'T LAST FOREVER,
IT WILL ALL EVENTUALLY BE OK.

SELF ♡ LOVE

You should be the greatest love of your life,
You are beautiful and deserve to be treated right;
For better or worse you should always put your
feelings first
from the moment you wake up until you go to
bed at night.
Occasionally write yourself the world's greatest
love letter,
Saying how special you are and that you deserve
good things and if you don't get them,
you deserve so much better.
Before you love anyone else, you need to
love yourself,
through sickness and health,
It's essential that you take care of your mental
and physical health.
The relationship you have with yourself can
be the greatest love story ever told;
Life is your adventure,
put yourself right at the centre,
Always love yourself when you are young
and when you get old.

You will get back up
each time you fall,
it's hard,
But you are special
and while you're alive
it's not impossible;
Don't ever give up
if you hit a brick wall,
when you find strength
you can break it down,
until it's nothing at all.

I Need . . .

I need to feel joy, I need a positive change;
I need to realise my potential instead of thinking that I'm going mental
or that I'm strange.
I need to stop trying to impress people, I need to impress myself instead;
I need to start believing that I've got nothing to prove to anyone in my head.
I need to stop saying 'Yes' all the time, I need to start saying 'No';
I need to know that I deserve any good things I get
and that I belong where I am, wherever I go.
I need times when I don't have to be anywhere at all or to answer to anyone,
I need to be less anxious about what the future may bring;
I need days when I just do nothing and do not have to worry about a single thing.
I need a good belly laugh, I need to act daft,
I need to take things lightly when I'm up shit's creek on a raft;
I need giggles and laughter, I need to be as happy as a happy ever after,
I need to be less serious when I'm face to face with drama and disaster;
I need to loosen my belt buckle, I need jokes and a chuckle;
I need to be tickled pink and less philosophical when I think,
I need cheeky innuendos with a bit of nudge nudge wink wink.
I need to find things funny and worry less about money;
I need to laugh so much that I split my sides,
I need to be as playful as playground rides;
I need more comedy and less tragedy,
I need the medicine of humour bottled up
and prescribed to me as a remedy.

Imposter Syndrome

I can't do this, I'm no good at it,
I feel like a fraud;
I just got lucky, I don't know what I'm doing,
So don't deserve accolades,
or any of the nice names I get called.
I'm not good enough, I should enjoy it while it lasts,
One day I will get found out;
I won't live up to expectations,
Good things will be erased during bad situations
and I will be left with nothing but doubt.

But I am good enough,
Any great things I have are not due to luck,
I work hard and I deserve to be rewarded with success;
I should accept compliments and praise,
I am marvellous in so many ways,
I'm not crazy, I'm just dealing with stress.
I am who I am,
I won't consider myself as a sham;
I have earned the right to be here
and to have a good home.
I need to love myself,
I should take care of my physical and mental health,
Yes, I'm imperfect but I won't be labelled as unworthy
by imposter syndrome.

AFTERNOON ASSURANCES

Randomly pick one of these affirmations,

Repeat it and keep it with you

Wherever you are and wherever you go;

If it doesn't suit you or the situation
you're in, please feel free to change it.

Just remember that you're special and
you really should know.

Why try to fit in if you were born to stand out? Shine with pride instead of hiding in a shadow of doubt.

It's okay to cry and let the tears fall from your eyes when your brain feels like a rain cloud.

If you screw things up try not to stress, lessons can be learned when you're cleaning up the mess.

Different languages spoken can cause a conversation of frustration, but our smiles are universal and they don't need any translation.

Any bad day can be improved significantly with a little bit of kindness and positivity. Try it. What's the worst that can happen if you do?

It's only you who suffers if you sacrifice what pleases you to always try to please others.

Value the thoughts, feelings and views from people who want the best for you.

The horizon might be out of reach, but you can still put yourself on the map.

Life isn't a piece of cake, but you should have a little peace for your own sake.

Sometimes life seems rubbish, but don't throw it away.

Don't listen to the people who judge you by giving imaginary scores, listen to those who encourage you with support and applause.

Believe in your own abilities and things will eventually fall into place.

As you chase your dreams you may fall, it's better than having no passion at all.

Tough times are temporary and so is pain; for rainbows to appear you need sunshine after rain.

The future can be bright, but it's difficult to see, if you're wearing rose-tinted glasses and obsessed with how things used to be.

Focus on the good things and the way forward when life becomes a blur instead of being over-critical about where and who you are.

There's really no way of knowing where you're going, but as long as you're in your boat just keep on rowing.

If you're fed up of performing the old same song and dance, break free from life's routine whenever you get the chance.

You're not being rude for not being in the mood.

Why do some people make other people feel insecure just to make themselves feel better? We are all better than that.

Maybe the time that you wish away will be a moment that you miss someday.

Life isn't a race; we all end up at the same place. Slow down and take your time.

People treat you the way they feel about you, words may say something else but actions can't always lie; if you don't feel appreciated or feel as if you're being taken for granted it's time for you to start thinking of saying goodbye.

On days of leisure just try to relax and do things that bring you pleasure.

You are not a burden, you are not a waste of space; there is only one of you and nobody can ever take your place.

Sadness isn't a moment of madness; we all need compassion to feel gratitude and gladness.

Work may drive you berserk and the world seems like a circus, but you are not a clown.

Only do what you can do and what you're comfortable with doing, never be afraid to ask for a helping hand; it's not down to you to exceed expectations, it's up to others to show empathy and to understand.

Don't keep it all in, speak your mind and use your voice; be proud to say 'this is who I am' and if somebody doesn't like you, don't worry, it's just their choice.

There's no real benefit in living a lie; some kind of therapy can help you get by.

Celebrity Collaborations

These incredible people have inspired us, entertained us, educated us, supported us, helped us and motivated us (and many other people) in so many ways and we had the honour of collaborating with them on these following poems. Each one of them is more than a celebrity.

They are absolute legends in our eyes and have experienced their own struggles and traumas in life, but have overcome their own obstacles to triumph in various ways; breaking taboos, smashing stigmas, bringing happiness, shining a light in the darkness, raising awareness about conditions, raising millions of pounds for charity and defying any perceived odds stacked against them.

Individually their achievements are far too many to list on this page, but they have shown that being deaf won't stop you from becoming a *Strictly Come Dancing* champion, having no legs won't stop you from breaking records and becoming a wrestler, having dyslexia won't stop you from becoming a successful entrepreneur, and being diagnosed with stage 4 cancer won't stop you from becoming a national treasure and saving other people's lives. We tried so hard to make one of Deborah James's wishes come true by campaigning to get her on to *Strictly*, but it didn't happen, but it did lift her spirits and make her happy. We are glad we played a part in getting Deborah a damehood. It's the very least she deserved. Her legacy will live on, and her star will shine forever.

We love every single one of these people who we have collaborated with. Check out their books, podcasts, TV and Radio appearances, live stage shows, festivals, self-help workshops and social media to see how amazing they are.

Zion Clark, Theo Paphitis, Nik and Eva Speakman, **Steven Bartlett,**
Katie Piper OBE, Fearne Cotton, Rose Ayling Ellis, Dame Deborah James.

NO FEAR, NO LIMITS, NO EXCUSES

A POEM BY ZION CLARK + ALL ON THE BOARD

YOU DON'T NEED TO HAVE FEET TO MAKE A STAND OR
TO LEAVE AN IMPRINT ON LIFE,
NO ONE SHOULD BE JUDGING YOUR SELF-WORTH, EXCEPT
FOR YOU;
YOU CAN BE YOUR OWN WORST ENEMY AT TIMES,
BUT YOU SHOULD ALWAYS BE YOUR OWN BEST FRIEND,
ANY SUCCESS AND HAPPINESS YOU GAIN
CAN HELP TO EASE THE PAIN
THAT YOU MAY GO THROUGH.

YOU WON'T ALWAYS BE IN THE MOOD OR FEEL MOTIVATED,
BUT YOU HAVE TO BE DISCIPLINED TO ACHIEVE GREATNESS,
IN TIME YOU WILL SEE
THAT THE CHALLENGES YOU FACE ARE MINUSCULE
COMPARED TO WHO YOU ARE
AND YOU CAN BECOME MORE MENTALLY STRONG;
LIFE IS YOUR ADVENTURE AND YOU SHOULD PUT YOURSELF
RIGHT AT THE CENTRE OF IT,
YOU CAN MAKE IT YOUR STORY
BY CHOOSING WHAT TO WRITE AND WHAT TO DO WITH IT,
WITH NO FEAR, NO LIMITS AND NO EXCUSES,
THERE WILL BE NO NEED TO DWELL ON THE THINGS YOU
MIGHT GET WRONG.

DYSLEXIA CAN BE A SUPERPOWER

A POEM BY THEO PAPHITIS + ALL ON THE BOARD

DYSLEXIA CAN BE A SUPERPOWER IF IT IS DEALT WITH IN A POSITIVE WAY,
LOOK AT THE PROBLEM, BREAK IT DOWN AND FIND THE ANSWERS,
THINKING OUTSIDE OF THE BOX IS PERFECTLY OKAY;
IF I DIDN'T HAVE DYSLEXIA, I'M PRETTY CERTAIN
THAT I WOULDN'T HAVE GOT TO WHERE I AM TODAY.
I SPENT A LOT OF MY SCHOOL LIFE DAYDREAMING AND LOOKING THROUGH THE WINDOW,
WONDERING TO MYSELF, 'WHY DO MY TEACHERS THINK I'M THICK?'
EVEN THOUGH THE SIMPLEST TASK WAS A CHALLENGE
MY BRAIN UNDERSTOOD I HAD TO LEARN TO USE WORKAROUNDS TO FIND A SOLUTION;
IT'S NO DISGRACE IF A BRAIN HAS TO GO ALL OVER THE PLACE
AND WORK HARDER TO COME UP WITH AN ANSWER,
IN MANY WAYS WHEN IT COMES TO PROBLEM-SOLVING,
VISUALISING AND UNDERSTANDING COMPLEX ISSUES,
HAVING DYSLEXIA CAN BE AN ADVANTAGE.
IT'S GOOD THAT AWARENESS HAS IMPROVED WITH A BETTER UNDERSTANDING,
LEARNING FROM MISTAKES, PROGRESS AND EVOLUTION.
THE PAST IS A SMALL SECTION OF OUR JOURNEY TO THE PRESENT
AND INTO A MUCH MORE INFORMED FUTURE,
TIME CAN BE ENLIGHTENING AND THERE IS SO MUCH SOCIETY CAN LEARN ALONG THE WAY.
THERE IS NO SUBSTITUTE FOR HARD WORK,
NOBODY JUST BREEZES THROUGH LIFE MAKING MONEY AND BEING SUCCESSFUL,
DYSLEXIA MAKES SOMEONE'S BRAIN WORK DIFFERENTLY TO OTHERS,
BUT THAT'S PERFECTLY OKAY.

PHOBIAS

A POEM BY <u>THE SPEAKMANS</u> + ALL ON THE BOARD

YOU WEREN'T BORN WITH A PHOBIA; PHOBIAS ARE IRRATIONAL FEARS,
THEY CAN BE 'SIMPLE' OR 'COMPLEX',
IT DOESN'T MATTER HOW LONG YOU'VE HAD YOUR PHOBIA FOR,
EVERY PHOBIA CAN BE OVERCOME;
PHOBIAS CAN CAUSE YOU TO WORRY, BE NERVOUS, ANXIOUS, ISOLATED AND LONELY,
SOMETIMES LEAVING YOU FEELING MISUNDERSTOOD, WEAK AND NUMB.

MOST PHOBIAS ARE CREATED IN CHILDHOOD
WHEN YOU DON'T HAVE THE LIFE SKILLS
TO MAKE SENSE OF AN UPSETTING SITUATION,
PHOBIAS CAN BE COPIED FROM A PARENT OR A CLOSE FAMILY MEMBER TOO;
SCARY, TRAUMATIC, CONFUSING OR EMBARRASSING EXPERIENCES CAN ALSO TRIGGER PHOBIAS,
YOU MAY AVOID CERTAIN PLACES, PEOPLE AND THINGS,
ADOPTING SAFETY BEHAVIOURS, SUPERSTITIONS
AND RITUALS FOR YOUR PHOBIA NOT TO COME TRUE.

YOU CAN FEAR ANYTHING, FROM THE DARK TO FLYING;
COMMON PHOBIAS INCLUDE SPIDERS, HEIGHTS,
SNAKES, CLOWNS, VOMIT AND DYING,
YOU CAN START TO FIX THE PROBLEM IF YOU RETRACE THE PHOBIA TO YOUR EARLIEST MEMORY;
AND BEGIN TO THINK TWICE,
TO REALISE THE VOICE INSIDE YOUR MIND IS GIVING UNHELPFUL ADVICE,
THEN YOU ARE NO LONGER A VICTIM AS YOU STRIVE FOR VICTORY.

SELF-DEVELOPMENT, PERSONAL GROWTH

A POEM BY STEVEN BARTLETT + ALL ON THE BOARD

THERE CAN BE NO SELF-DEVELOPMENT WITHOUT SELF-AWARENESS,
YOU CAN READ AS MANY BOOKS AS YOU LIKE,
BUT IF YOU'RE UNABLE TO READ YOURSELF,
YOU WILL NEVER LEARN A THING;
SELF-BELIEF IS A CONCEPT THAT'S GROSSLY MISUNDERSTOOD,
YOU CAN ACHIEVE IT IF YOU WANT IT AND IT CAN MAKE YOU FEEL GOOD,
IT'S ALL ABOUT CONFRONTING AND OVERCOMING THE BELIEFS ABOUT
YOURSELF CAUSED BY YEARS OF SUBCONSCIOUS CONDITIONING.

INTENTION IS NOTHING WITHOUT ACTION AND ACTION IS NOTHING
WITHOUT INTENTION,
PROGRESS HAPPENS WHEN INTENTIONS AND ACTIONS BECOME THE SAME;
IT'S MORE IMPORTANT TO LIVE UP TO YOUR OWN EXPECTATIONS, RATHER
THAN ANYBODY ELSE'S,
DON'T LET YOUR PAST EXPERIENCES PREVENT YOU FROM STRIVING FOR
WHAT YOU BELIEVE;
EVERYONE BUYS BOOKS, BUT FEW EVER READ THEM,
EVERYONE WANTS GROWTH, BUT FEW ACCEPT PAIN,
EVERYONE WANTS TO BE HAPPIER, BUT FEW EVER CHANGE TO MAKE IT
HAPPEN,
EVERYONE WANTS RAINBOWS WITHOUT ANY RAIN;
LIFE HAS A FUNNY WAY OF GIVING GRATEFUL PEOPLE EVEN MORE THINGS
TO BE GRATEFUL FOR,
WITH GRATITUDE AND SELF-APPRECIATION FOR WHAT THEY HAVE AND
ANYTHING THEY ACHIEVE.

FEELING SEEN IN SOCIETY

A POEM BY KATIE PIPER + ALL ON THE BOARD

BEING ABLE TO BE OURSELVES,
NO MATTER WHAT OUR APPEARANCES ARE LIKE,
IS SO IMPORTANT AND HEALING,
LIFE IS MADE EASIER FOR PEOPLE LIVING DIFFICULT LIVES
WHEN TABOOS ARE REMOVED
TO GIVE A FULL REPRESENTATION OF SOCIETY;
IT'S ESSENTIAL FOR PEOPLE TO BE EDUCATED
NOT TO ASK INTRUSIVE QUESTIONS
OR TO STARE AT PEOPLE WHO ARE VISIBLY DIFFERENT;
IT'S NOT ABOUT CHANGING HOW SOMEBODY LOOKS,
IT'S ABOUT CHANGING CERTAIN BEHAVIOURS
AND HOW SOME PEOPLE SEE.

ONLINE ABUSE, TROLLING, BULLYING, INSULTS AND DISGUSTING COMMENTS
CAN MAKE LIVING SO HARD FOR SOMEONE WHO IS BURNT,
VISIBLY DIFFERENT, DISFIGURED OR SCARRED;
NOBODY SHOULD EVER TRY TO VALIDATE THE NEGATIVES IN THEMSELVES
BY TRYING TO TEAR OTHERS DOWN,
OR JUSTIFY CRUEL WORDS AND THE DAMAGE THEY CAN DO;
IT CAN FEEL LIKE A LONG, LONELY JOURNEY
TRYING TO REJOIN SOCIETY
AND FINDING A PATH TO LIVING A NORMAL LIFE
FOR SOMEONE FINDING IT DIFFICULT TO LEAVE THEIR HOUSE,
THEIR ORDEAL CAN BE HELPED WITH KINDNESS,
AND FOR PEOPLE TO TRULY THINK
BEFORE THEY WRITE OR OPEN THEIR MOUTHS,
WE SHOULD NEVER JUDGE ANYONE OR THINK WE KNOW SOMEBODY'S STORY
IF WE DON'T REALLY KNOW WHAT THEY'VE BEEN THROUGH.

WICKED WORDS

A POEM BY <u>FEARNE COTTON</u> + ALL ON THE BOARD

NOTE ALL THE TIMES YOU'VE SAID IN YOUR HEAD
THAT YOU'RE NOT GOOD ENOUGH;
JOT THEM DOWN, TALLY THEM UP,
CATCH THEM WITH A LASSO AND LAY THEM TO BARE;
WHEN YOU LOOK AT THE WICKED WORDS THAT HAVE CAUSED YOU TROUBLE,
SEE THEM AS DIRT THAT HAS FORMED A PILE OF ACERBIC RUBBLE;
YOU ARE BETTER THAN THE SLURS, PUT DOWNS, ASSUMPTIONS AND THE
WICKED WORDS OF PEOPLE BEING CRUEL AND UNFAIR.

HOW MUCH TIME HAVE YOU WASTED BEING DECEIVED, BELIEVING THE
THOUGHTS AND WICKED WORDS OF OTHERS?
COLLECTING THEM LIKE SHELLS ON A BEACH,
KEEPING EACH ONE IN YOUR POCKET AND LETTING THEM WEIGH YOU DOWN;
DON'T LET OTHER PEOPLE'S OPINIONS BECOME FASTENED BUTTONS, TRAPPING
YOU INSIDE A COAT YOU DIDN'T CHOOSE TO WEAR,
DON'T PONDER OVER PEOPLE'S POISONOUS POINTS OF VIEW THAT DIRECT YOU
AND THE FAITH IN YOURSELF TO EVERY DEAD-END STREET IN YOUR TOWN.

WHOSE WICKED WORDS DO YOU CARRY AROUND UPON YOUR BACK?
WHO TRIED TO DAMAGE YOUR DREAMS,
BREAK DOWN YOUR SELF-ESTEEM BY FOCUSING ON WHAT YOU LACK?
WHOSE ANNOYING, SOUL DESTROYING VOICE FOLLOWS YOU LIKE A SHADOW
AND AFFECTS THE THINGS YOU DO?
SIFT THROUGH GENTLER ADJECTIVES AND SOFTER VERBS
AND CHOOSE TO BE KIND TO YOUR MIND BY PINNING BETTER SENTIMENTS
TO YOUR HEART,
YOU HAVE ALWAYS MATTERED SO DON'T LET WICKED WORDS SHATTER YOU
AND BREAK YOU APART;
PEOPLE'S WICKED WORDS SAY MUCH MORE ABOUT THEM THAN THEY DO
ABOUT YOU.

DINNER TABLE SYNDROME

A POEM BY ROSE AYLING ELLIS + ALL ON THE BOARD

EXPERIENCING THE 'DINNER TABLE SYNDROME' AS A DEAF PERSON
CAN CAUSE FEELINGS OF FRUSTRATION,
TRYING TO BECOME NUMB TO IT MAY MAKE YOU FEEL SLIGHTLY
BETTER,
BUT IT DOESN'T IMPROVE THE SITUATION;
PRETENDING TO UNDERSTAND WHAT'S GOING ON
AND LAUGHING WHEN OTHERS ARE LAUGHING TOO,
BECAUSE YOU WANT TO BE INVOLVED IN THE CONVERSATION;
THE SOUND OF SILENCE CAN SEEM DEAFENING
TO SOMEONE FEELING INVISIBLE AND SECLUDED IN SOCIAL ISOLATION;
IT'S A RELIEF WHEN SOMEONE AT THE DINNER TABLE QUIETLY
NOTICES
AND MAKES AN EFFORT WITH THEIR COMMUNICATION;
SOME DEAF PEOPLE LIP READ AND SOME USE SIGN LANGUAGE,
EVERYONE IS DIFFERENT,
ASK WHAT'S BEST FOR THEM SO WORDS ARE NOT LOST IN
TRANSLATION.

DON'T BRUSH A DEAF PERSON ASIDE,
IF THEY ASK YOU TO REPEAT,
REPEAT CALMLY WITH PATIENCE AND THE SAME INTONATION;
IT CAN BE EXHAUSTING AND OVERWHELMING TRYING TO KEEP UP,
JUST BECAUSE SOMEONE IS DEAF THEY SHOULDN'T FEEL DESOLATION,;
LET'S WORK TO BRING EVERYONE TOGETHER WITH EDUCATION;
DEAF PEOPLE SHOULDN'T JUST BE SEEN AS BEING DEAF,
THEY HAVE FEELINGS, THOUGHTS, OPINIONS AND EMOTIONS LIKE
EVERYONE ELSE,
WE CAN LEARN SO MUCH FROM EACH OTHER WITH OPEN MINDS,
KINDNESS AND CONSIDERATION.

REBELLIOUS HOPE

A POEM BY DAME DEBORAH JAMES + ALL ON THE BOARD

IF ME AND CANCER WERE IN A BOXING RING, I WOULD KNOCK IT OUT,
BUT IT'S A COWARD AND IT HIDES INSIDE OF ME;
I'M NOT BRAVE OR A SOLDIER, SO HOW CAN I EVEN FIGHT IT,
WHEN THE BATTLE IS WITH SOMETHING I CAN'T SEE?
SOME DAYS ARE GOOD AND SOME ARE BAD, I GET HAPPY AND I GET SAD,
I DON'T FEEL LIKE I'M A HERO BEING STRONG BY SURVIVING
AND STANDING TALL;
WHEN I'M SCARED IT'S TOUGH TO SHOW A BRAVE FACE,
MY EMOTIONS ARE ALL OVER THE PLACE,
I'M IN A WAR AGAINST MY ORGANS WHERE THE WINNER WINS
NOTHING AT ALL.
JUST BECAUSE I HAVE A TUMOUR IT DOESN'T MEAN I DON'T HAVE
A SENSE OF HUMOUR,
I WILL DANCE IN THE RAIN, CHA CHA THROUGH THE CHAOS AND
SALSA THROUGH THE STORM;
PLEASE DON'T THROW YOUR ARMS AROUND ME THINKING I
NEED SYMPATHY,
I MIGHT JUST NEED YOUR ARMS TO KEEP ME WARM.
EVEN THOUGH CANCER ISN'T FUNNY,
WE STILL LOVE TO LAUGH AND TRY TO HAVE FUN,
TO LIVE THE BEST WE CAN IS ALL WE WANT TO DO;
HAVING CANCER DOESN'T STOP US LOVING WHAT WE DID BEFORE
THE DIAGNOSIS,
CREATING MEMORIES WITH LOVED ONES AND WISHING FOR DREAMS
TO COME TRUE,
CANCER CAN AFFECT AS MANY AS ONE IN TWO;
IF IT'S NOT ME IT COULD BE YOU.
IT'S A CONDITION FOR WHICH WE CAN NEVER TRULY BE PREPARED;
EARLY DETECTION CAN BE A PREVENTION,
THERE IS SUPPORT WAITING FOR YOUR ATTENTION,

IT'S PERFECTLY NORMAL TO FEEL
STRESSED, FED UP AND SCARED.
WE ALL HAVE ONE THING IN COMMON:
CANCER IS A UNIVERSAL PROBLEM,
IT DOESN'T DISCRIMINATE OR CARE FOR
WHO IT TAKES HOLD;
IF WE KEEP DONATING TO CHARITY TO FUND
RESEARCH AND TECHNOLOGY,
ONE BEAUTIFUL DAY IN THE FUTURE,
CANCER WILL BE TREATED LIKE A
COMMON COLD.
THOSE WHO DIED DIDN'T FAIL, THEY DIDN'T
BATTLE LESS THAN SURVIVORS LIVING NOW,
THEY ARE NOT VICTIMS, THEY ARE NOT
WEAK AND THEY ARE NOT LOSERS, TOO;
CHECK YOURSELF REGULARLY, TAKE CARE
PHYSICALLY AND MENTALLY,
LIVE YOUR LIFE WITH REBELLIOUS HOPE –
AND DON'T FORGET TO CHECK YOUR POO.

Dame Deborah James
1981–2022

GOOD
EVENING

Home

There are many wonderful places in the world that make me happy, but after a while I just want to return to my happiest: home.

Home is what it's all about. Surrounded by your favourite things. A place where you can rest and recover. A place where you can be yourself. A place where you can do what you love doing. It's the place you truly miss if you're away from it for too long.

The happiest moment in the school or work day is 'home time'. Even if you've been on an amazing holiday, there's still something nice about getting back home. Home is a place where you should feel safe, but for so many people in the world that isn't the case. A home should be filled with love. A home should *be* love.

I spend so much of my life wanting to get home and trying to get home. But a home doesn't have to be a place: it can be someone you love. No matter where you are in the world or how lost you may feel, as long as you are with someone you love, then everywhere is home. Hearts become homes.

Like Dorothy in *The Wizard Of Oz* said, 'There's no place like home,' and she's absolutely right. She was wrong about the ruby slippers, though – as much as I've clicked together my own they have never taken me home in an instant. (Disclaimer: I don't own any ruby slippers…yet.)

A HOUSE ISN'T A HOME

A HOUSE ISN'T A HOME
UNTIL THERE'S LIFE AND LOVE
TO MAKE IT COME ALIVE;
THE FRONT DOOR IS A MOUTH
THAT WELCOMES PEOPLE IN
BY SAYING 'HELLO' AS THEY ARRIVE.
THE WINDOWS ARE EYES,
THE PAINTWORK AND THE WALLPAPER ARE SKIN,
THE WALLS THAT HOLD UP THE ROOF ARE THE BONES WITHIN;
THE BOILER IS THE HEART,
THE ELECTRICITY IS THE BRAIN,
THE DRAINAGE PIPES ARE THE DIGESTIVE SYSTEM
AND EVERY WIRE IS A VEIN.
A HOUSE WILL OCCASIONALLY BREATHE THROUGH A CHIMNEY
OR AN EXTRACTION FAN
AND SEND ITS BREATH INTO THE SKY ABOVE;
ATTICS, WARDROBES, CELLARS AND DRAWERS
ARE THE PLACES WHERE PRECIOUS MEMORIES ARE STORED,
BUT A HOUSE ISN'T A HOME
UNTIL THERE'S LIFE AND LOVE.

Social anxiety

I've had social anxiety most of my life and it's been one of the hardest things to get through because it feels so determined to isolate me no matter what I need or want. It makes invitations so easy to decline. I get a momentary relief when I do that feels HUGE, yet very quickly afterwards I realise that I've lost more than I've gained, and I've not stepped forward in my fight to rid myself of this thing.

The day we removed our masks my level of anxiety was through the roof. There were interviews and articles and all that jazz; I was petrified. I still am every time invitations come through, but because of the good I know our book and work brings to so many I've had a stronger reason to accept those invitations. It's helped me to accept invitations to talk on stage, be interviewed, have selfies with and meet people I would have been nervous about in the past. I still have anxiety but I know I've got a way through that's worth something and I know afterwards that each time has brought me immense happiness and a sense of purpose I would not have gained had I declined them. It's an ongoing journey. Maybe one day, the more I do this the less difficult that journey will become.

UNDERGROUND

<u>THE NEWS TODAY</u>

THERE'S A LOT OF BAD NEWS GOING ON.
DON'T FOCUS ON IT. ALSO, WHATEVER YOU
HAVE NEVER SEEMS TO BE ENOUGH.

<u>IN OTHER NEWS</u>

YOU ARE AWESOME. YOU CAN SWITCH OFF
THE NEWS. YOU CAN FOCUS ON DOING
SOMETHING YOU ENJOY. YOU CAN PHONE
LOVED ONES. THERE ARE AMAZING
PEOPLE DOING AMAZING THINGS. IT WON'T
ALWAYS BE THIS WAY.

UNDERGROUND

MAYBE YOU FEEL RUFF, PAW-LY OR HUSKY,
PERHAPS A HOT DOG AND HOT UNDER THE COLLAR
BECAUSE YOU'VE BEEN WORKING LIKE A DOG,
OR MAYBE YOU FEEL LIKE A SAUSAGE DOG CHASING
YOUR OWN TAIL
AND BARKING UP THE WRONG TREE.
POSSIBLY YOU FEEL LIKE YOU'RE UNLUCKY IN PUPPY LOVE.
TRY TO CHEER PUP AND BE PAW-SITIVE.
NOTHING CAN KEEP A GOOD DOG DOWN,
FETCH YOURSELF SOME TREATS TO PUT IN YOUR DOGGY BAG
AND DO THINGS THAT MAKE YOUR TAIL WAG.
EVEN THOUGH PAW-FECTION DOESN'T EXIST
YOU'RE NEVER TOO OLD TO LEARN NEW TRICKS AND THERE·S
PLENTY OF LIFE IN YOU YET.
GO FOR WALKIES AND DON'T ROLL OVER WHEN IT'S
RAINING CATS AND DOGS.
PLEASE REMEMBER THAT NO STORM LASTS FUR-EVER
AND EVEN IF TODAY IS NOT YOUR DAY AND PERHAPS
TOMORROW ISN'T YOUR DAY EITHER,
EVERY DOG HAS ITS DAY AND SO WILL YOU.

Hope you're feline okay.
I'm not letting the cat out of the bag by saying no matter how cool you are you will never be as cool as a cat. I'm just kitten around.
We are definitely cooler than dogs though.
There may be days when you don't feel like you've got the cream and maybe you don't feel like grinning like a Cheshire Cat
because you don't always land on your feet, but it's okay.
Sometimes you may feel like a scaredy cat,
thinking like you look like something I've dragged in
or anything that you try seems to end up in a catastrophe. Nobody's purr-fect.
There's no need to be a copycat of somebody else.
Don't just be like the mice and play when cats are away,
find something you enjoy doing every day, as long as it's not swinging cats around rooms.
Life is too short to be playing any cat and mouse games with anybody though.
I may have nine lives, but you don't, so live your best life and know that anything is paw-sible because you are the cat's whiskers.

BATHS

BATHS ARE FANTASTIC AND CAN BE SO RELAXING,
WITH A BIT MORE TIME ON YOUR HANDS THEY ARE A PLEASURE TO LIE IN,
WHEN THE RUSH OF LIFE IS TOO MUCH TO HANDLE
THERE'S NOTHING QUITE LIKE SCENTED CANDLES AND A TUB FULL OF BUBBLES;
IT'S HARD TO GET OUT OF ONE WHEN YOU'RE IN IT,
EVERY TIME YOU ATTEMPT TO GET OUT YOU THINK 'JUST ONE MORE MINUTE,'
A PLUNGE WITH A SPONGE AND A RUBBER DUCK
CAN HELP YOU FORGET ABOUT YOUR TROUBLES.

SOAKING FOR TOO LONG CAN SHRIVEL YOUR SKIN UP LIKE A PRUNE
WHILE YOU'RE GETTING CLEAN,
BUT BATHS ARE THE PERFECT PLACE TO TAKE TIME OUT
AND READ A NOVEL OR A MAGAZINE,
THEY HELP YOUR MUSCLES AND ACHES TO RECOVER
AND LEAVE YOU FEELING SNOOZY;
THERE MAY BE TIMES WHEN YOU FEEL WINDY
AND YOU CAN CREATE YOU'RE OWN JET STREAM
TO ADD TO YOUR PERSONAL JACUZZI.

BE PROUD

AT TIMES IT MIGHT HAVE SEEMED IMPOSSIBLE,
BUT EACH AND EVERY SINGLE TOUGH TIME YOU HAVE GOT THROUGH;
YOU ARE STRONGER THAN YOU THINK YOU ARE,
DURING THE DARKNESS YOU SHINE LIKE A STAR
AND YOU SHOULD TRULY BE SO PROUD OF YOU.
BE PROUD OF WHO YOU ARE AND HOW YOU HAVE GOT SO FAR,
BE PROUD THAT YOU HAVE GOT THROUGH EACH DIFFICULT SITUATION
AND YOU'RE STILL ALIVE;
BE PROUD THAT YOU GOT BACK UP
EVERY TIME YOU GOT KNOCKED DOWN,
NO MATTER HOW LOST YOU ARE YOU ALWAYS FIND A WAY TO SURVIVE.
MAYBE YOU FEEL BETTER THAN YESTERDAY,
PERHAPS YOU FEEL WORSE TODAY THAN YOU DID THIS TIME LAST YEAR;
TRY TO RELAX AND FACE THE FACTS
THAT IN LIFE THERE ARE SETBACKS,
YOU MIGHT NOT BE ON THE RIGHT TRACK,
BUT BE PROUD THAT YOU'RE STILL HERE.
YOU MAY HAVE BEEN BRUISED AND FELT BATTERED,
PHYSICALLY KNACKERED AND MENTALLY SHATTERED,
YOU HAVE ALWAYS MATTERED AND YOU SHOULD HAVE SPOKEN
WHEN YOU FELT BROKEN AND DAMAGED;
EVEN THOUGH YOUR PRIDE TRIED TO HIDE WHAT YOU FELT INSIDE
DURING THE SHOCKS OF THE GHOST TRAIN AND THE UPS AND DOWNS OF
A ROLLERCOASTER RIDE,
YOU SHOULD FEEL PROUD THAT YOU GOT THROUGH
AND SOMEHOW MANAGED.

BABIES & CHILDREN IN HEAVEN

IF YOU COULD HAVE BEEN SAVED BY LOVE AND PRAYERS
YOU WOULD HAVE LIVED FOR ETERNITY,
INSTEAD WE ARE LEFT ASKING QUESTIONS IN OUR HEADS
AND IMAGINING WHAT KIND OF FINE PEOPLE
YOU WOULD HAVE TURNED OUT TO BE.
JUST BECAUSE YOU WERE TAKEN FROM THIS EARTH
AND OUR WORLDS TOO SOON
IT DOESN'T MEAN THAT YOU DIDN'T EXIST;
YOUR DEPARTURE LEFT US EMPTY AND BROKEN-HEARTED,
YOU WILL BE FOREVER LOVED AND ALWAYS MISSED.
WE MAY NOT GET TO HOLD YOUR HANDS
OR HOLD YOU IN OUR ARMS,
BUT WE SHALL HOLD YOU IN OUR HEARTS WITH ENDLESS LOVE;
WE KNOW FAMILY AND FRIENDS IN HEAVEN
WILL GUIDE YOU AND LOOK AFTER YOU,
AS YOU PLAY IN PARADISE WITH ANGEL WINGS,
UP IN THE SKY ABOVE.
YOU WILL NEVER GROW OLD, YOU WILL NEVER FEEL THE COLD,
YOU WILL NEVER HAVE WORRIES OR EXPERIENCE
SORROW, FEAR AND PAIN;
UNTIL TIME BRINGS US BACK TOGETHER
WE WILL LOVE YOU FOREVER,
ONE DAY IN THE FUTURE WE WILL SEE YOU AGAIN.

Grief

There is no wrong or right way to grieve. Cry if you need to cry. You will always miss the person you've lost and the pain of them not being there anymore will always be with you, but it becomes more bearable as time goes on. We all have to grieve at some point in our lives. The only thing that's guaranteed to happen to us when we are born is that we will die.

Take as long as you need. There are no instructions on how to grieve and there is no timescale on when you will feel better, but please know that one day you will feel better. Grieving is having so much love for someone who is no longer with you and not knowing what to do with that love. They may not be with you physically, but if you carry them in your heart and your mind they will be with you forever.

If there is any comfort to be taken it's that they are in a much better place where nothing can ever hurt them. Some people believe in Heaven and some people don't. I do believe in Heaven. I know that when this life is over I will be reunited with my loved ones. I found them in this life and I shall find them in the next life too.

As lonely as it feels, you are not alone. There are people who you can talk too if you are struggling with grief. Everybody grieves at some point.

 BOARD GAMES

GUESS WHO? FEELS LIKE THEY ARE LOSING A GRIP ON
A BATTLESHIP,
THE GAME OF LIFE CAUSES ANXIETY
THAT HAS A MONOPOLY OVER ME AND GIVES ME STRESS;
MY BRAIN IS SOMETIMES IN A SCRABBLE
AND MY MIND IS AN INCOMPLETE JIGSAW PUZZLE,
I'M LIKE ONE OF THE HUNGRY HUNGRY HIPPOS
IN NEED OF AN OPERATION TO REMOVE A MUZZLE,
ANY TIME I HAVE A DOWNFALL IT'S BEST TO GET IT
OFF MY CHESS.
I'M LOOKING FOR A CLUEDO ON A TRIVIAL PURSUIT,
WITH EVERY RISK I TAKE I'M ROLLING THE DICE
FEELING LIKE I'M CAUGHT SHORT IN NEED OF A LUDO
AND THE SNAKES AND LADDERS COULD BE A WATER CHUTE,
EXCLUDING DRAUGHTS I FEEL DAFT AS I'M SPUN AROUND BY
A TWISTER ON THE FLOOR;
KERPLUNK GOES EACH TEARDROP FROM MY EYE LIKE A
DRIPPING TAP,
CHECKERS OUT WHEN I BUCKAROO! AND I LAND IN
A MOUSE TRAP,
LIFE ISN'T A GAME
AND IS SOMETIMES NO PRETTY PICTIONARY,
THAT'S WHY HUMANS NEED TO CONNECT FOUR.

BREAKING UP

Love should kill the pain, but the bitter pill was hard to
swallow and now it's dissolved,
It's so difficult to be divided,
especially if there are children involved;
Arguing over things that don't matter,
two hearts have fallen apart
and the pieces have scattered,
Good times and good memories are not good enough
when looking through rose-tinted glasses that have
shattered.
It's like you're grieving for someone still living and you don't
know how to feel,
Embarrassment delays you telling friends and family,
Because it would make the situation real;
The things that used to charm you
might now get on every nerve,
Well-meaning friends may want to gather around you
and help you find somebody you deserve.
It's nobody's fault if lovers fall out of love
and a relationship has run its course,
Unless cheating and threatening behaviour has led to
breaking up, separation or divorce;
There are reasons why an ex is an ex,
Don't view those past relationships through rose-tinted
glasses or blurry specs;
Instead of dwelling on broken relationships with regret,
Think of all the wonderful people
that you haven't met just yet.

PETS

PETS ARE THERE FOR YOU WHEN YOU'RE FELINE RUFF,

GOING MUTTS OR NEED CHEERING PUP,
THEY ARE PURRFECT FRIENDS AND WILL FUREVER KEEP YOU COMPANY;
THEY NEVER RABBIT ON AT YOU OR DIG THEIR CLAWS IN,
UNLESS THEY WANT FEEDING, STROKES OR TO GO FOR WALKIES,
8 OUT OF 10 CATS ARE NEVER GUINEA PIGS OVER THE REMOTE CONTROL
WHEN WATCHING THE TV.

IF YOU FEEL PAWLY AND AS SICK AS A PARROT
OR THE ROUTINE OF LIFE IS A HAMSTER WHEEL,
THEY CAN MAKE YOU HAPPY WITH THE LITTLE THINGS THEY DO;
FROM LASSIE VEGAS TO BARKINGHAM PALACE,
IF YOU'RE A PUPTOWN GIRL OR A DOWNTON TABBY,
IF YOU LOVE YOUR PETS YOUR PETS WILL LOVE YOU TOO.

musical me

IT'S CLASSICAL OF ME
TO FIND IT HARD TO SETTLE,
MY HEART IS BEATING THE RHYTHM
OF A MILITARY MARCHING DRUM
AND MY BRAIN FEELS LIKE HEAVY METAL
I WANT TO BE AS STRONG AS A ROCK,
BUT I JAZZ FEEL LIKE I'M READY TO POP;
IN MY SOUL I FEEL LIKE GRIME AND RAP
AND I DON'T WANT TO DANCE,
IT'S EASY LISTENING TO SOMEONE SAY
LIFE'S A JUNGLE, BUT GIVE IT A CHANCE,
INDIE END, SOMETIMES I JUST WANT THE VOLUME
TURNED DOWN
OR FOR THE MUSIC TO STOP.

You can't choose your family

We can't choose who we have as our family, but if we are lucky enough to be related to good, loving people, then that is everything.

A family who will love you for who you are, who will always put a roof over your head, will forgive you when you make mistakes, will sell everything they own if they had to just to make sure you eat and who want the very best for you is an absolute blessing. You feel exactly the same way about them too and wouldn't think twice about sacrificing your life for theirs.

Yes, you may argue at times, but you find a way to forgive each other. Some families don't though and carry on a family feud for years or for the rest of their lives.

It's so sad that some people in this world unfortunately don't get the loving family that they deserve. When they should be hugged, they are hit; when they should be kissed, they are kicked. It is heartbreaking. There are also loving people in the world who would give anything to be able to have children, but for various reasons they can't.

Families get together if it's a wedding, a funeral or someone's landmark birthday or anniversary. (Dads, grandads and uncles occasionally show off their best dance moves on these occasions. Not necessarily at funerals, though that would be some funky funeral going on.) One of the family members is guaranteed to say at some point, 'It's a shame that we all don't get together more.' And it probably is. For some, though, these occasions are more than enough.

We do get a couple of strange ones (it's never us though, is it) in our families, but nevertheless, they are still family. It's crazy (well, at least it is to us) to think that our family tree goes all the way back to when fish started growing legs (we're not very scientific) and started walking about on Earth.

How do you get on with your family?

DOMESTIC ABUSE

ANYBODY CAN BE THE VICTIM OF AGGRESSION,
IT CAN BE PHYSICAL AND PSYCHOLOGICAL TOO;
FROM A BROKEN SPIRIT AND A BROKEN MIND
AND LOW SELF-ESTEEM
TO SCARS AND BRUISES BLACK AND BLUE.

THERE IS NO EXCUSE FOR INFLICTING A VICTIM
TO DOMESTIC ABUSE;
IF YOU ARE THREATENED OR HURT BY
SOMEBODY'S VIOLENCE,
REACH OUT FOR HELP AND PLEASE DON'T
SUFFER IN SILENCE.

GRIEVING

When I'm crying I can dry my tears but I can't stop it
from raining in my heart;
At times I can hold myself together,
but there are moments when I fall apart.
You would want me to continue life after you've died;
I know you are there even if I can't see you by my side.
If I didn't love you so much it wouldn't hurt so much
but I do;
I thought about you yesterday
and I will think about you tomorrow too;
I must confess as time goes by the pain hurts a little less
but I will never stop thinking of you.
I know I will never really get over it
I just want to get through it,
I know it may take a while;
Of course I will always miss you,
But there will come a day when instead of crying
I will cherish every memory of you and smile.
We never know what hug will be the last goodbye,
We never know how many tears we will cry;
Eventually acceptance comes and we stop questioning why.
Heaven will need back the people we love someday;
Make memories with those we love
And may those memories never fade away.

I'M NOT FRYING,
I'VE HADDOCK WITH
FEELING BATTERED
WHEN MY CHIPS ARE DOWN;
I KNOW A FISH
THAT'S AN ANGEL,
I KNOW A FISH
THAT'S A CLOWN.
OH MY COD! LIFE'S TOO SALT
FOR US NOT TO BE FEELING
GRAVY AND AT EASE;
AT ANY TIME AND ANY PLAICE
WHEN I'M LOST AT SEA
MY BRAIN IS LIKE MUSHY PEAS.
I'M A GOOD SOLE,
SO DON'T MULLET OVER
IF YOU'RE HERRING
FISHY RUMOURS THAT I DON'T CARE,
WHEN WE HAVE
A LOT ON OUR PLATES
DON'T SKATE AROUND, WE ALL
NEED SALMON TO BE THERE.

FAMILY

IF IT'S RAINING, IF IT'S SNOWING
OR YOU NEED PROTECTION FROM A STORM,
I PROMISE I WILL GIVE YOU SHELTER,
MY HEART WILL BE YOUR HOME
AND MY LOVE WILL KEEP YOU SAFE AND WARM;
IF THERE ARE DARK CLOUDS AND THE SKY IS GREY
OR THE SUN IS OUT, IN A SKY SO BLUE,
I PROMISE WHATEVER THE WEATHER
I WILL ALWAYS BE THERE FOR YOU.
I LOVE YOU AND I WANT YOU TO UNDERSTAND,
THAT I WILL NEVER BE EMBARRASSED
OR TOO OLD TO HOLD YOUR HAND.
WHEN I FEEL SAD AND NEGATIVE,
I CHEER UP KNOWING THAT YOU'RE MY RELATIVE;
WHEN LIFE MAKES ME FRUSTRATED,
I STILL FEEL BLESSED THAT WE ARE RELATED;
BEING WITH YOU WILL ALWAYS BE MY FAVOURITE MEMORY,
IT'S A PLEASURE BEING CONNECTED TO YOU
AND I'M CERTAIN YOU WOULD AGREE,
I WANT YOU TO KNOW THAT YOU MEAN THE WORLD TO ME,
FATE PUT US TOGETHER AND MADE US FAMILY.

CHEATED ON

I DON'T NEED TO HEAR THE REASONS WHY YOU CHEATED;
ALTHOUGH I'VE LOST ALL TRUST IN YOU, I'VE NOT BEEN DEFEATED.
OF COURSE I FEEL EMBARRASSED,
BUT WHEN I THINK ABOUT IT, I'M MORE EMBARRASSED FOR YOU;
YOUR TWISTED LIES DISGUISED YOUR DISLOYALTY OR WANDERING EYES,
SO YOU SHOULDN'T BE SURPRISED IF I QUESTION WHAT WAS TRUE.
OF COURSE I'M GOOD ENOUGH, BUT WHEN THINGS GET ROUGH,
QUITE CLEARLY YOU'RE NOT EVEN ENOUGH FOR YOU;
WELL DONE FOR MAKING ME BELIEVE THAT YOU LOVED ME
WITH THE DECEITFUL THINGS YOU SAY AND DO.
WITHOUT A DOUBT MY CONFIDENCE WAS ROCKED
AND I FELT KNOCKED OUT,
WHAT A MISTAKE I MADE
TELLING MY FAMILY AND FRIENDS YOU WERE PERFECT FOR ME;
INSTEAD OF BEING UNFAITHFUL BY STABBING ME IN THE BACK,
YOU SHOULD HAVE SHOWN SOME RESPECT AND SET ME FREE.
IT'S NOT HARMLESS FLIRTING IF IT CAUSES SOMEONE TO BE HURTING,
WONDERING WHERE THE SECRETS LEAD TO NEXT;
LOVE ISN'T A GAME WHEN A PARTNER IS BETRAYED BY A PLAYER,
FROM TOUCHING AND KISSING ANOTHER
TO DELETING EVERY DEVIOUS TEXT.
I WILL LISTEN TO THE SAD LOVE SONGS, AND THEN MOVE ALONG,
A BROKEN HEART IS NEVER BEYOND REPAIR;
DON'T GIVE ME ANY EXCUSES
BECAUSE YOU KNEW WHAT YOU WERE DOING,
IF OUR RELATIONSHIP WAS A CAR
YOU CRASHED IT ON THE ROAD TO RUIN,
I DESERVE BETTER THAN YOU AND FOR SOMEONE TO TRULY BE THERE.

CHILDLESS
NOT BY CHOICE

PEOPLE WHO LONG TO BE PARENTS

BUT CAN'T HAVE CHILDREN FOR VARIOUS REASONS

SHOULDN'T HAVE TO HEAR INSENSITIVE SENTENCES LIKE

'YOU MAY REGRET IT,'

'THE CLOCK IS TICKING,'

'YOU'RE SO LUCKY NOT TO HAVE ANY KIDS,'

OR 'WHAT'S WRONG WITH YOU?';

TO BE CHILDLESS, NOT BY CHOICE, CAN LEAVE A BODY AND SOUL

OVERWHELMED BY SADNESS AND GRIEF.

FROM AN ACHING BROKEN HEART TO AN EMPTY STOMACH,

FEELING LIKE A FAILURE WITH WASTED LOVE

OR ROBBED BY FATE, THE INVISIBLE THIEF,

THERE ALWAYS SEEMS TO BE A MISSING PIECE

COMING OUT
WHENEVER YOU'RE READY

YOU DON'T NEED TO EXPLAIN WHO YOU ARE
AND WHO YOU LOVE TO ANYONE,
THERE IS NO HURRY IN ANNOUNCING OR LABELLING YOUR SEXUALITY;
HOPEFULLY ONE DAY IN THE FUTURE
COMING OUT WILL BE LIKE TALKING ABOUT THE WEATHER,
INSTEAD OF CAUSING SOMEBODY STRESS AND ANXIETY.

COMING OUT ISN'T FOR EVERYBODY,
TAKE YOUR TIME AND WAIT UNTIL YOU'RE TRULY READY,
THIS IS YOUR STORY AND IT NEEDS NO EXPLANATION;
THOSE WHO TRULY LOVE YOU WILL ACCEPT YOU
AND LOVE YOU FOR BEING YOU,
THEY WILL STAND BY YOUR SIDE TO BREAK ANY STIGMA
AND DESTROY DISCRIMINATION.

WE SHOULD CELEBRATE AND EMBRACE WHO WE ARE,
WOULDN'T IT BE NICE TO LIVE IN A WORLD WHERE COMING OUT
DOESN'T TAKE COURAGE AND STRENGTH AND CAN AFFECT
A PERSON'S MENTAL HEALTH;
WHEREVER YOU ARE ON YOUR JOURNEY,
YOU ARE VALID AND YOU MATTER,
LOVE IS LOVE, BE WHO YOU ARE AND BE PROUD OF YOURSELF.

Cruel and negative comments
    can affect somebody's life
      and their state of mind;
Everyone has an opinion,
    but, one thing we should agree on
      is that it's always best to
        BE KIND.

 # Dear Loved One In Heaven

I miss you so much, I thought I would write you a letter,
I will never get over you, I wouldn't want to, I just want to feel better.
I would give up everything I have for one more chance
To talk to you, hug you tightly and have one last dance.
I love it when you visit me in my dreams,
but when I wake up I'm quite sad;
But I cherish the precious memories of you
and the good times we had.
I know you want me to be happy and carry on
And I promise you I will, but a part of my heart will always grieve;
Some people on Earth don't think there's an afterlife,
But I know you are in Heaven and I truly believe.
Is Heaven everything you expected it to be?
How wonderful does it feel to be with past friends and family?
Do you find out the meaning of life?
And does paradise have beautiful places to explore?
Even though you can't keep me company,
I take great comfort knowing that where you are now
you will always be safe, you no longer feel sorrow or pain
and nothing can hurt you any more.
Until the day arrives when we are reunited in heaven above,
I will live my life like you would want me to
and remember you with love,
You are in a better place, but I still wish you were here;
I will have good days and bad days and there may be moments I cry,
There will be times when I smile when you pop up in my mind,
I will love you forever and because you are living in the next life,
I know you will wait for me until I've lived my life on Earth
realising that death is something that I shouldn't fear.
Love, Me

DECLINING INVITATIONS

IF YOU'RE IN A BAD WAY,
DON'T FEEL GUILTY ABOUT SOMETIMES WANTING TO BE LEFT ALONE
OR NOT ANSWERING THE PHONE,
DON'T FEEL BAD ABOUT DECLINING INVITATIONS,
CANCELLING PLANS OR LETTING PEOPLE DOWN;
THERE'S NO NEED TO COME UP WITH LIES AND ELABORATE EXCUSES,
JUST TELL THE TRUTH IF YOU'RE NOT IN THE MOOD TO MEET UP
FOR A SOCIAL OCCASION, GOSSIPING, DRINKS AND FOOD;
WHEN YOU'RE NOT FEELING ALRIGHT,
A NIGHT INDOORS CAN OCCASIONALLY SUIT YOU MORE
THAN A NIGHT ON THE TOWN.
YOU DON'T FEEL LIKE MEETING UP WITH ANYBODY
SO YOU CANCELLED GOING OUT TONIGHT;
YOU DON'T WANT TO LIE OR MAKE EXCUSES,
YOU JUST WANT TO TELL THEM THAT YOU'RE NOT FEELING QUITE RIGHT.
IRRATIONAL THOUGHTS FILLED WITH 'WHAT IFS',
A HEART BANGING FAST AND WORRIED IT WILL EXPLODE,
SICK OF APOLOGISING KNOWING THAT SOCIALISING WOULD BE GOOD FOR
YOU,
BUT AT THE MOMENT YOU'VE GOT AN UNWANTED DATE WITH ANXIETY,
THE WEIGHT OF THE WORLD IS SO HEAVY
AND IT CAN BE FRIGHTENING UNTIL YOU LIGHTEN THE LOAD.

Fears

Fears are a little bit weird. I'm scared of spiders, but I can't tell you where my fear came from. Maybe it was from a film that I saw featuring spiders being all spidery. A spider has never hurt me or broken my heart. I find the way they move quite sinister, calculating and creepy, but they are just being spiders. I'm sure they find the way I move a little weird too. I even had the police knock on my door one evening because a neighbour reported that someone was being attacked in my flat. It was just me screaming at a spider.

When people have a fear of flying, have they ever been involved in an actual plane crash? How many people were scared of going in the water when *Jaws* (the movie) came out in the 1970s? Clowns have got it pretty hard too; all they want to do is make people laugh with their big shoes and glitter, driving about in their unreliable cars and yet, how many find them creepy? That fear definitely comes from watching movies with killer clowns in. Who would be a clown in this day and age? The world is a circus though.

Some fears are because somebody has been through a traumatic event and that's completely understandable. We can all conquer our irrational fears with patience, time and understanding. Do you have a fear? Why do you have your fear?

Do You Have An Addiction, Or Does Your Addiction Have You?

I drank for happiness and became unhappy,
I drank for joy and just became sad;
I drank to be social and became argumentative,
I drank to relax, but the headaches and shakes drove me mad.
I drank for friendship and made myself enemies,
I drank for courage and ended up afraid;
I drank for confidence and it left me doubtful,
I drank to forget and remembered every bad choice I made.
I drank for sleep and would wake up so tired,
I drank for strength and I only felt weak;
I drank to taste heaven and I just went through hell,
I drank to make conversation and just slurred when I tried to speak.
I drank because I needed to and I didn't know why,
I drank because I was addicted and it left me on my knees;
I stopped drinking to save myself and for my loved ones,
I was trying not to be selfish as I was battling my disease.
I didn't want to be labelled as my condition,
I have a name and I'm human too;
At this moment in time, do you have an addiction?
Or does your addiction have you?

LITTLE REMINDERS OF OUR LOVED ONES IN HEAVEN ABOVE,
WHO HAVE LEFT US BEHIND,
CAN HAPPEN IN THE FORM OF WHITE FEATHERS
FALLING TO THE FLOOR FROM NOWHERE
AS MEMORIES POP UP IN THE MIND.
CERTAIN HABITS, SAYINGS AND SMELLS TRIGGER RECOLLECTIONS,
JUST LIKE SONGS THAT PLAY ON THE RADIO;
RETRACING THE FOOTSTEPS OF THE PAST
AND THE PLACES THEY WOULD GO.
HOME VIDEOS BRING THEM BACK TO LIFE,
JUST LIKE SOUVENIRS OF YEARS GONE BY
CAPTURED IN A PHOTOGRAPH;
CONVERSATIONS WITH RELATIONS OF STORIES AND SITUATIONS,
REMEMBERING THE WAY THEY USED TO LAUGH.
SOMETIMES THEY BRIEFLY VISIT US IN OUR DREAMS,
BUT IN OUR HEARTS FOREVER THEY WILL STAY;
LITTLE REMINDERS OF THEM
FOR THE REST OF OUR LIVES,
UNTIL WE MEET UP AGAIN
SOME BEAUTIFUL DAY.

LOOKING FOR LOVE

I DON'T NEED SOMEBODY WHO HAS EVERYTHING,
I JUST WANT SOMEONE WHO WILL DO ANYTHING FOR ME;
MAYBE I'VE BEEN LOOKING IN THE WRONG PLACES,
IF LOVE WANTS ME IT KNOWS WHERE I WILL BE.
PATIENTLY WAITING CAN BE QUITE FRUSTRATING
WHEN YOU'RE READY FOR LOVE;
IT'S BEST NOT TO GET STRESSED,
BECAUSE I DESERVE THE VERY BEST
WHEN CUPID SHOOTS HIS ARROW FROM ABOVE.
I WANT SOMEONE THAT TREATS ME LIKE A PRIORITY,
I WANT SOMEONE WHO JUST WANTS MY COMPANY;
I WANT SOMEONE WHO LOVES ME FOR BEING ME,
I WANT SOMEONE TO KNOW THAT WE ARE MEANT TO BE.
SWIPING LEFT AND SWIPING RIGHT TO FIND A BEST FRIEND
TO CUDDLE AT NIGHT,
THE UNCERTAINTY OF EVERY DATE
TO SEEK A SOULMATE MIGHT NOT BE GREAT,
BUT IT'S AN AUDITION FOR MARRIAGE MATERIAL;
EVERYONE HAS BAGGAGE AND PERFECTION DOESN'T EXIST,
I'M ON THE MARKET TO FIND A PARTNER
I NEVER KNEW I MISSED
AND WHEN THEY COME INTO MY LIFE,
THEIR EYES WILL REFLECT SOMETHING BEAUTIFUL.

HOLD ON TO HOPE

HOLD ON TO HOPE,
KEEP IT CLOSE TO YOUR HEART
AND IT WILL HELP YOU TO COPE.
HOLD ON TO HOPE TIGHT,
IN THE DARKNESS YOU CAN SQUEEZE IT
AND IT WILL WORK LIKE A LIGHT,
SO WHEN YOU CAN'T SEE THE WAY
YOU CAN FEEL THAT THINGS WILL BE ALRIGHT.
HOLD ON TO HOPE AND DON'T LET IT GO,
IT CAN COMFORT YOU
AND SHOW YOU THAT YOU'RE NOT ALONE WHEN YOU'RE LOW.
HOLD ON TO HOPE LIKE A TEDDY BEAR,
IF YOU KEEP IT BESIDE YOU
WHEREVER YOU'RE TRYING TO GET TO
IT WILL REMIND YOU THAT YOU'RE HALFWAY THERE.
HOLD ON TO HOPE
AND IF LIFE GETS COLD IT WILL KEEP YOU WARM,
RAISE IT OVER YOUR HEAD
AND IT WILL PROTECT YOU FROM EVERY STORM.

WHEN I FEEL TIMES ARE HARD
AND THEY MESS WITH MY HEAD,
I JUST NEED THE SOFTNESS
OF A PILLOW
AND THE COMFORT OF MY BED;
WHEN I FEEL I'VE HAD ENOUGH
OF EVERYDAY DRAMAS,
I JUST NEED
THE TV REMOTE CONTROL
AND THE COSINESS OF MY PYJAMAS.
WHEN I FEEL EDGY, ANNOYED,
TIRED AND STRESSED,
I JUST NEED TIME OUT FOR ME
TO RECOVER AND REST;
WHEN I FEEL LIKE A JOKE
WHO NEVER GETS THE LAST LAUGH,
I JUST NEED TO RELAX
AND HAVE BUBBLES IN A BATH.

I'M SORRY
IF I'VE NOT
REPLIED TO YOUR MESSAGE
OR DIDN'T ANSWER YOUR CALL,
FOR MY OWN SAKE
I NEED SOME TIME AND SPACE;
I'M NOT IGNORING YOU,
I LOVE HAVING YOU IN MY LIFE
AND I PROMISE
I'M ALWAYS HERE FOR YOU,
BUT AT THE MOMENT
MY HEAD IS NOT
IN THE RIGHT PLACE.

I'm Panicking, It's Petrifying

I'm panicking, it's petrifying,
I know it's anxiety and my brain is lying;
It's telling me danger is approaching
And I'm on the verge of dying.
I'm not sure who I am anymore,
If it's fight or flight,
I'm frightened and I feel like I'm frying.
I'm trying, I'm trying, I'm tired of trying,
It's exhausting when I want to be still,
But my mind is racing time and frantically flying;
I want to scream at the horizon,
I'm on the edge of breaking down and crying.
Crushed by the rush of it all,
Paranoia reminds me of strangers' eyes prying,
Tongue-tied and on the inside
I'm hung up high and dry,
With heart palpitations sounding like planets colliding.
My oh my, why is it always me?
I know others feel the same,
But in a moment of my madness it's hard to see,
I know I need to breathe.
Yes, it's lonely and scary,
It reaches a peak of making me feel helpless and weak
And then it stops intensifying and starts subsiding,
Even though I've survived every panic attack I've ever had,
It doesn't make it any less stressful and terrifying.

Friends

Friends are the people we would choose to have as family members if we had the choice; the people we want to have adventures with, who make us laugh and listen to us when we need to talk. Good friends are hard to find, just like treasure, but what an absolute gem they are if they are found.

I've never found it easy to make friends. I've spent years without friends of any kind, and I've experienced trauma with friends and because of the loss of them. In school I was more or less an outcast so I had to be my own friend and learn how to be those missing voices of support every growing child longs for. When I left school, I gained the freedom to do this outside of the confines of the school playground or classrooms. I could go to the cinema a lot, I exercised and I got creative and eventually even learned to laugh at myself.

The friends I have connected with have had a profound impact on my life and I can now honestly say life is so much better with friends. I hope that, over the years, I've given my friends as much in return as they have given me: perspective, support, humour, escapism, memories that last and so much more.

Whether you have friends or not, don't forget to be a friend with yourself too.

IF I COULD REWIND ⟵◻◻◻◻ THE TIME

IN HEAVEN THERE IS NO PHONE RECEPTION
OR INTERNET CONNECTION,
SO I WILL SEND YOU LITTLE MESSAGES IN MY MIND;
I MISS YOU AND I'M GRIEVING
BUT FOR SOME REASON IT WAS YOUR TURN
TO MOVE FORWARD ON TO YOUR NEXT ADVENTURE
AND LEAVE THIS LIFE BEHIND.

I NEVER WANTED YOU TO GO,
I KNOW YOU NEVER WANTED TO LEAVE
AND IF WE COULD CHANGE THE END
WE WOULD HAVE SAID A PROPER GOODBYE;
IF I COULD REWIND THE TIME
I WOULD HAVE TOLD YOU JUST HOW MUCH I LOVE YOU,
I HOPE YOU HEAR THOSE WORDS IN MY MIND
WHEN I THINK ABOUT YOU
AND LOOK UP TO THE SKY.

189

If You See Your Life As A Movie

If you see your life as a movie
make the soundtrack to it groovy,
Get a good cast who will support you,
Because you're the leading star;
You can choose how to act
and react in any situations,
You can add special effects,
Costumes and animations,
But if you change locations
don't forget where you're from and who you are.
In a world of special effects,
Sometimes you may not feel so fantastic;
There are people who disguise reality with lies
by using technology and C.G.I.,
And at this present time you may be using
Sellotape and sticky back plastic.

IN CONTROL WITH THE TV
REMOTE IN YOUR HAND

ESCAPING REALITY WITH ENTERTAINMENT IS COMPLETELY ALRIGHT;
IT'S NOT A SIN IF YOU BINGE WATCH TV
FROM THE MORNING TO THE NIGHT.
IF YOU'RE NOT FEELING GROOVY YOU CAN GET LOST IN THE
PLOTS OF SOME MOVIES FOR HOURS ON END;
WHEN YOU SPEND TIME
WATCHING THE LIVES OF OTHERS ON THE SCREEN
EACH CHARACTER CAN FEEL LIKE A FRIEND.
WHEN LIFE GETS TOO MUCH
IT'S FINE TO SWITCH OFF FROM THE WORLD
AND SWITCH THE TV ON;
MILLIONS OF PEOPLE AROUND THE WORLD DO THE SAME THING
AND THEY UNDERSTAND,
YOU CAN'T ALWAYS TIDY UP MESS
OR CONTROL ANY OUTSIDE STRESS
THROWN UP BY THE 21ST CENTURY,
BUT WHEN YOU'RE INSIDE YOUR HOME,
YOU'RE IN CONTROL WITH THE TV
REMOTE IN YOUR HAND.

INFERTILITY

Inside it may feel like little pieces of hope are dying,
But it's love that offers courage to persist and keep trying.
The heartbreak can be too much to take when you've done
everything you can do;
It's understandably frustrating and debilitating
when it seems like everyone else is getting pregnant
and having children instead of you.
To other people it seems to happen so easily and it's tough
to understand,
All you want is a little version of you in your life
to love and to hold their hand.
It's an emotional rollercoaster that can cause so much pain,
both mental and physical;
Money gets in the way, but it's a small price to pay
for somebody who wants the chance to raise a little miracle.
You would love them so much if you could,
But it's not happening and you don't know why;
You would fill their heart with wonder,
pass on your knowledge
and sing them every lullaby;
You would protect them from danger
and dry up every tear they cry;
You would love them so much if you could,
But it's not happening and you don't know why.

IT'S MORE IMPORTANT TO LOVE YOURSELF

IT'S BETTER TO BE SINGLE
AND TO BE ON YOUR OWN,
RATHER THAN BEING WITH SOMEONE
WHO MAKES YOU FEEL LONELY
AND AS IF YOU'RE ALONE.
BEING IN A RELATIONSHIP
DOESN'T NECESSARILY MAKE YOU HAPPIER,
BEING SINGLE DOESN'T MEAN
THAT YOU'VE BEEN LEFT UPON THE SHELF;
BEING WITHOUT A PARTNER
DOESN'T MEAN THAT YOU'RE A FAILURE
OR THAT LOVE IS A DISASTER,
BEING IN LOVE WITH SOMEONE
CAN BE WONDERFUL,
BUT IT'S MORE IMPORTANT TO LOVE YOURSELF.

Fun

Whatever you enjoy doing, do it as much as you can, as long as it doesn't hurt anyone, get you into trouble or put yourself in unnecessary danger.

Also make sure you don't have to break the bank or break into a bank to be able to afford the kind of fun that you have in mind.

Life gets a bit serious sometimes and can just seem like it's all work, work, work. We have to find a time to play. Growing up doesn't mean we have to stop having fun.

What do you like doing for fun?

🚇 UNDERGROUND **JEALOUSY**

The grass seems greener on the other side of the fence
If it feels to you like everybody else is having all the fun;
Left in the shade, questioning every decision that you've made,
just waiting for a chance to shine in the sun.
In our hearts and minds jealousy can create anger and hate,
Normally because of what someone has
and what somebody doesn't possess;
It would be nice if we could all feel real admiration,
Instead of envy and frustration,
Jealousy is good for nothing and just causes bitterness and stress.
From gloating at failures and mistakes
to compliments with hidden insults,
Diminishing achievements, belittling success,
Bullying, trolling, backstabbing and gossiping too;
We can challenge ourselves not to compare ourselves
and what we have with other people,
If you're jealous of someone
it's highly likely there is someone jealous of you.

NON-FICTIONAL FRIEND

SOME CHAPTERS OF YOUR BOOK
MIGHT BE DIFFICULT TO READ AND WRITE,
BUT, WHAT'S WRITTEN IN THOSE PARAGRAPHS
IS NOT HOW YOUR STORY WILL END;
WHEN YOU HAVE SOMEONE IN YOUR LIFE
WHO DOESN'T JUDGE YOUR COVER
OR WALK AWAY AS YOU TURN THE PAGE,
YOU HAVE FOUND THE PERFECT DESCRIPTION
OF A NON-FICTIONAL FRIEND.

ONE

IF I HAD ONE MINUTE LEFT TO LIVE I'M NOT SURE
WHAT I WOULD SAY OR DO,
ALL I KNOW IS THAT I WOULD WANT TO SPEND THOSE
LAST SIXTY SECONDS OF MY LIFE WITH YOU;
IF I HAD ONE DAY LEFT TO LIVE I'M NOT SURE HOW IT
WOULD BE,
ALL I KNOW IS THAT I WOULD WANT THOSE TWENTY-
FOUR HOURS TO JUST BE YOU AND ME;
IF I HAD ONE WEEK LEFT TO LIVE I'M NOT SURE WHAT
COULD BE DONE,
ALL I KNOW IS THAT I WOULD SPEND THOSE SEVEN
DAYS LETTING YOU KNOW
THAT YOU HAVE ALWAYS BEEN THE ONE;
IF I HAD ONE YEAR LEFT TO LIVE I'M NOT SURE WHAT
I WOULD PLAN TO DO OR HOW TO START,
ALL I KNOW IS THAT I WOULD WANT TO SPEND THOSE
TWELVE MONTHS WITH YOU
AND NOT LET ANY DAY KEEP US APART.

Pets

The moment pets bless us with their presence and move into our homes they immediately become family members. They really are wonderful. They could certainly teach the human race lessons in how to behave – except for when they sniff each other's backsides and poo on the carpet. Mind you, there are some freaky humans in the world that probably do that too.

Pets are the very best friends that you can ever have. They love you and expect nothing from you, apart from being fed and being given the occasional treats. They will never talk about you behind your back. They are always up for cuddles and strokes. They genuinely make you feel loved. They never intentionally break your heart, but they do break hearts when they pass away and go to pet heaven. I know my heart has been broken (as well as my family's hearts) whenever we have lost a pet. They are not just pets, they are family. Depending on when we get our furry – or scaly – friends, we see the whole of their lives and it's so sad saying goodbye to them.

If there are any pets that are reading this, we just want to say, 'Thank you for being you,' (At some point we will get that translated into dog language, cat language and all of the other animal languages.) A massive shout out to the pets on Earth and the ones in Heaven. We absolutely love you all.

PANIC ATTACKS
CAN BE BEATEN

PANIC ATTACKS CAN COME OUT OF NOWHERE,
THEY DON'T CARE IF IT'S DAY OR NIGHT;
AS TERRIFYING AS THEY ARE THEY EVENTUALLY PASS,
AND EVERYTHING WILL BE ALRIGHT.
IF YOU DO SOME RESEARCH TO TAKE THE MYSTERY AWAY,
THERE IS HELP IN WHAT YOU WILL FIND;
THERE ARE EXPLANATIONS FOR WHAT HAPPENS IN THE BODY,
AND WHAT GOES ON INSIDE THE MIND.
PLEASE KNOW THAT YOU ARE NOT ALONE IN THIS WORLD,
MILLIONS OF OTHER PEOPLE GET THEM TOO;
FIND A METHOD TO USE WHEN YOU'RE HAVING ONE,
AND SOMETHING WILL WORK FOR YOU.
EVEN THOUGH THERE MAY BE NO DANGER OR THREAT,
PANIC ATTACKS CAN PREPARE US FOR ACTION;
TRY SOME DEEP BREATHING, IT CAN BE SO RELIEVING,
OR SOLVE PUZZLES AND TRY MENTAL DISTRACTION.
THERE ARE REASONS BEHIND WHAT WE ARE FEELING,
LET'S LOSE THE WEIGHT OF THE WORLD FROM OUR BACKS;
IT'S HARD TO KEEP CALM, BUT A PANIC ATTACK CAN NOT HARM,
TALK TO SOMEONE AND PLEASE TRY TO RELAX.

Sofa So Good (An Ode To A Sofa)

So far, so good, sofa, so good,
Upholstery for my lethargy made from fabrics, steel and
plastic, but mostly wood,
It holds you up horizontally or vertically
if you're feeling down;
Lying there like the king or queen of your castle without
a crown.
In the space between each arm
is a space for me to keep calm;
It cradles me and keeps me company
While I'm reading or if I have the TV remote control
glued to my palm.
Safe on cushions of foam that remind me I'm home,
The comfort of a sofa can be sat on, but never beat;
The backsides of guests
may be impressed by their cosiness,
In between the soft cracks surprises arise from
welcomed coins to the odd misplaced sweet.
Often upon them our furry friends
leave souvenirs of fur,
Sofas are furniture that become a part of the family
making cats purr and other pets will concur.
They are great to snuggle up on while daydreaming,
pretending you're on a cosy canoe
lazily going down-stream,
Occasionally looking through the window
watching what kind of weather the sky has in store;
They are great for watching your favourite TV on
while having snacks or eating a TV dinner,
It doesn't matter which shape or size you choose,
every couch is a winner,
They will be there for you when you're feeling ill and will
save you from sitting on the floor.

Suicide

Please, please, please if you are reading this and you are thinking that life is not worth living and you want it all to come to an end, don't do it.

It may not seem like it right now, but there will be better days and brighter days. They may not come tomorrow, next week or next month, but those better days will come. You are not alone and there are plenty of people and organisations out there who will listen to you and help you. You will get through these bad times.

If the bad times are storms, they do eventually pass. All storms do. If the storm comes back, it will pass again. One day you will look back on your present self and be proud that you stuck around.

We have lost friends to suicide, and we know that they would still be here if they could have opened up with their feelings and talked to people. Please talk as much as you want to and need to.

SOME PEOPLE DON'T
ALWAYS SAY
'I LOVE YOU',
IT DOESN'T MEAN
THAT THEY DON'T CARE;
THEY MAY SAY
OTHER THINGS LIKE,
'I GOT THIS FOR YOU',
'CALL ME WHEN YOU
GET HOME', 'BE SAFE'
AND 'IF YOU NEED ME
I WILL BE THERE'.

THE CINEMA EXPERIENCE

Mesmerised by the magic of movies
during matinees and evening screenings
with no life distraction,
Brains engaged by the performances, special effects,
lights, camera and action.
The best place to see a film is on the big screen,
Not an airplane, a tablet or a phone;
Nothing beats the anticipation
when the lights go down in the auditorium,
Surrounded by other people sharing the immersion of the
cinema experience together, alone.
Jaws drop to floors from the surround sound of epic scores
and the roars of monsters and dinosaurs;
Escape from reality by defying gravity
on an adventure through space;
Fall in love with people falling in love
in beautiful locations upon the silver screen;
Travel on an incredible journey without leaving your seat
to other worlds and galaxies far, far away
and any time and place.
Superhero spectacles, marvellous musicals,
amazing animations,
Fantastic fantasies, delightful dramas,
award-worthy inspirations for all moods and occasions.
There can be a childlike excitement
waiting for the next blockbuster to arrive;
Thrills, chills, gasps, laughter and tears,
The smell of popcorn, the sights, sounds and atmosphere,
Larger-than-life memories are created and adored
and that's why we need to keep the joy of the cinema
experience alive.

Relationships

In a good relationship you should be able to be lovers and best friends. You should be able to have a secret language and joke around. There should be kisses at all times of the day that say to one another, 'You're the one for me,' with hugs that make you feel like you're home in each other's arms.

In a relationship you should be able to completely be yourself and know that your partner loves you for who you are. There should be plenty of daft, playful moments and when things get a bit serious, you should have each other's backs. A certain stare that you give one another should lead to a smile.

In a good relationship you should realise that the two of you are not perfect, but you are perfect for one another. Nights in cuddled up on the sofa watching movies and eating snacks become more appealing than going out. You burst with pride at each other's achievements. Your favourite word in the world is your lover's name. You become each other's carers in times of illness and need. You have arguments, but you try to sort them out as soon as you can. No matter where you are in the world, as long as you are with one another, everywhere feels like home. You should be comfortable with one another, but never to the point where you take one another for granted or you start taking advantage of each other. Early on in a relationship you try your best to stifle farts or disguise them; as the relationship progresses it can be quite fun to drop a comedy fart out of the blue occasionally (or maybe that's just us).

Your partner's happiness should mean more to you than your happiness. You should want each other as much as you need each other and need each other as much as you want each other. Through good times and bad times you should stick together like you're a two-person team (because you are) and it's the pair of you against the world – not in a competitive way, just a kind of 'if you upset my lover I won't be very happy at all' way.

Relationships are awesome if you're with THE ONE, but if you're with someone that abuses you or makes you feel lonely, even when you are together, as hard as it can be you need to get away. Obviously, some relationships do come to an end because of love dying or someone dying, but the relationship happened because it was meant to happen, for whatever reason.

You deserve to be loved. If you are not in a relationship, then you should love yourself. Actually, you should love yourself even if you are in a relationship. You are always in a long-term relationship with yourself, from the moment you are born to the moment you die. Make sure you love yourself.

THERE'S NO NEED TO FEAR DEATH

THERE'S NO NEED TO FEAR DEATH,
WE ALL EVENTUALLY DIE;
EVERYONE WE KNOW, EVERYBODY FAMOUS
AND EVERY STRANGER THAT PASSES BY.
IT'S THE ONLY THING IN LIFE THAT'S GUARANTEED,
DEATH IS AS NATURAL AS BIRTH;
AS SAD AS IT SEEMS, EVERY FAMILY AND FRIEND
HAS A STORY THAT HAS A BEGINNING AND AN END,
THE FINAL CURTAIN IS CERTAIN
FOR EVERY LIVING PERSON ON EARTH.
LIFE IS A JOURNEY
THAT HAS VARYING DISTANCES FOR EVERYBODY
BUT DEATH IS THE FINAL DESTINATION,
WE ALL REACH IT THROUGH ILLNESS, TRAGEDY OR OLD AGE;
WHEN THERE IS NO MORE ROAD TO TRAVEL,
WE STEP OUT OF THE CAR,
THE SOUL GETS SET FREE FROM A BODY
THAT HAS BEEN IT'S CAGE.
BEFORE YOU WERE BORN, IN EFFECT YOU WERE DEAD,
DO YOU MISS YOUR LOVED ONES
WHEN YOU'RE SLEEPING IN BED?
THERE WILL BE NO MORE PAIN, HEARTBREAK OR MISERY
AFTER YOU BREATHE YOUR FINAL BREATH;
UNTIL YOUR FINAL DAY ARRIVES,
LIVE LIFE AND LOVE THE PEOPLE AROUND
YOU WHILE YOU'RE ALIVE,
TRY TO STOP WORRYING ABOUT WHAT WILL HAPPEN
AND PLEASE KNOW THAT
THERE'S NO NEED TO FEAR DEATH.

PLEASE DON'T FEEL LIKE YOU NEED TO
'MAN UP', 'WOMAN UP' OR WHATEVER KIND OF
UP THERE IS. YOU ARE <u>NOT</u> WEAK, YOU ARE
TIRED FROM BEING STRONG.
IF YOU FEEL LIKE CRYING, THEN PLEASE CRY.
IT'S OKAY TO CRY. ASKING FOR HELP
IS NOT GIVING UP, IT'S SAYING THAT YOU
DON'T WANT TO GIVE UP.
DON'T BOTTLE UP, OPEN UP AND
NEVER GIVE UP. PLEASE TALK AS WELL.
TALKING WILL HELP TO SAVE LIVES.

BULLIES & TROLLS

WHAT IS THE ROLE OF A BULLY OR A TROLL IN SOCIETY?
IS IT TO BE AN ANNOYING VOICE THAT CAUSES SOMEONE
MISERY AND ANXIETY;
HONESTLY, WHAT IS THE POINT
OF GETTING UP SOMEBODY'S NOSE
OR PUTTING A NOSE OUT OF JOINT?
WHO KNOWS WHAT IS GOING ON IN SOMEBODY'S MIND;
IT'S HEARTLESS TRYING TO DESTROY LIVES
AND IS MUCH MORE PRODUCTIVE BEING KIND.
IS IT A CRY FOR ATTENTION
OR A NEED OF WANTING TO BE HEARD?
INSULTS CAN BE REVOLTING, START A WRITING
REVOLUTION,
INSTEAD OF LAUGHING AT YOURSELF AND PLOTTING EVERY
HATEFUL WORD.
WHAT IS ACHIEVED? BE CREATIVE INSTEAD;
SCROLL PAST THEM, RESTRICT THEM, REPORT THEM,
DELETE THEM,
JUST IGNORE THEIR COMMENTS AND POISONOUS WORDS,
AND DON'T LET THEM GET INSIDE YOUR HEAD.

WHATEVER MAKES YOU HAPPY

LISTEN AND DANCE TO MUSIC YOU LOVE,

EXERCISE, TAKE A WALK OUTSIDE WITH NATURE
AND MAKE SHAPES FROM THE CLOUDS UP ABOVE;
GET LOST IN A BOOK, WATCH FILMS AND TV SHOWS
THAT MAKE YOU LAUGH,
RECALL HAPPY MEMORIES IN PHOTOGRAPHS
AND RELAX IN A BUBBLE BATH;
HAVE A CHAT WITH FRIENDS DRINKING ALCOHOL,
COFFEE OR TEA,
STROKING A PET CAN CHILL YOU OUT,
SO CAN MEDITATION, YOGA AND CREATIVITY;
HAVE A MASSAGE, PLAY GAMES, TRY COOKING AND A HEALTHY DIET,
TIDY UP, TRAVEL, KEEP A DIARY AND COME UP WITH A DOABLE PLAN;
WHATEVER MAKES YOU HAPPY DO IT AS MUCH AS YOU CAN.

UNDERGROUND WHEN YOU DIED

WHEN YOU DIED I FELT LIKE MY HEART HAD BEEN RIPPED APART,
MY FUTURE PLANS HAD BEEN RIPPED UP,
I WAS LOST AND EMPTY INSIDE,
IT SEEMED LIKE TIME WAS NO LONGER RELEVANT
AND AS IF THE CLOCK HAD STOPPED;
THE WORLD WAS STILL SPINNING AROUND
AND LIFE WAS STILL GOING ON FOR OTHER PEOPLE,
WHILE I WAS LIVING IN MY MIND
I FELT BROKEN AND MY SMILE HAD DROPPED.
HOW CAN OTHER PEOPLE BE FEELING HAPPY?
HOW CAN THEY BE LAUGHING?
THIS WORLD IS NOT THE SAME FOR ME
NOW THAT YOU'RE NOT HERE
AND IF YOU HAD BEEN IN THEIR LIVES
THEY WOULD CERTAINLY BE MISSING YOU;
I WILL NEVER GET OVER YOU,
BUT YOU WILL ALWAYS BE IN MY HEART
AND IT'S TIME TO START BELIEVING,
WITH EVERY DAY THAT PASSES THERE WILL BE LESS TEARS AND
A LITTLE LESS GRIEVING,
AT SOME POINT IN OTHER PEOPLE'S LIVES
THEY WILL BE TRYING TO DEAL WITH WHAT I'M GOING THROUGH
AND MISSING SOMEBODY THEY LOVE TOO.

YOU WERE MORE THAN A PET

Thank you for keeping me company for the whole of your life,

I loved you from the beginning to the end;

We spoke different languages,

but you always understood me,

You were more than a pet,

you were also my best friend.

You knew exactly what I needed

at any time of day,

When I felt the world didn't understand;

We shared so many moments together,

I will love you and miss you forever,

I know if it was possible you would have always held my hand.

BIRTH
TRAUMA

THOUSANDS OF WOMEN A YEAR EXPERIENCE BIRTH TRAUMA
AND SO MANY WOMEN AND THEIR PARTNERS CAN BE LEFT
                        TRAUMATISED BY A TRAUMATIC CHILDBIRTH,
FROM SEEING A BABY IN DISTRESS, SEVERE BLOOD LOSS, URGENT SURGERY
                        INTENSE PHYSICAL AND EMOTIONAL PAIN;
IT CAN BE HEARTBREAKING AND DIFFICULT TO BOND WITH A BABY
                        FOR A WOMAN WITH POSTNATAL PTSD,
RELATIONSHIPS WITH PARTNERS AND FAMILY MAY SUFFER
                        UNDER THE INCREDIBLE STRAIN.

EVERYBODY NEEDS SUPPORT TO RECOVER FROM TRAUMA,
A BODY AND MIND NEEDS TIME TO HEAL AND GROW STRONG,
IT CAN BE A LONG AND LONELY WALK THROUGH A PERSONAL HELL;
CARING FOR YOURSELF TRULY MATTERS
WHEN YOU FEEL PHYSICALLY, EMOTIONALLY AND MENTALLY SHATTERED,
THERE'S NO DISGRACE IF YOU NEED TIME AND SPACE
                        TO THINK ABOUT YOURSELF AS WELL.

STROKES

Phone 999 or the emergency services number wherever you are in the world to request an ambulance,
If you suspect you or someone else is having a stroke;
The symptoms may subside or disappear as you're waiting for an ambulance,
But, it's important to go to hospital for an assessment and not treat it as a joke.

Strokes usually begin suddenly and from person to person the symptoms and signs may vary,
But there are certain symptoms of a stroke we can recognise;
From numbness and weakness in one arm and not being able to lift the arms, not being able to talk,
Slurred speech and seeming confused,
It may be hard to smile, the face may have dropped on one side
And there may be a drooping of the mouth and the eyes.

Other potential symptoms may be dizziness, confusion, a sudden loss of eyesight or a blurring of vision,
Paralysis of one side of the body, difficulty understanding what others are saying and a sudden extremely painful headache that feels like no other;
There may be problems with co-ordination and balance, a loss of consciousness and swallowing can be a difficult challenge,
It's important that we recognise the signs of a stroke and that we are there to help others to recover.

EVENING ENCOURAGEMENTS

Select an affirmation at random
from the following pages,

Repeat it like a favourite song
until you believe it;

Today possibly hasn't been your day,

But you are truly amazing in so many ways.

If you have a dream, there's no
reason why you can't achieve it.

As tough as life can be, it has never stopped you; 100 percent of the time you have always got through.

Whenever and wherever there are glimmers of hope, you will find a way to cope.

At any point in life you can rewrite your story, find a new direction and reroute yourself to a path of glory.

When it happens, nothing hurts quite like rejection, but in hindsight it might have happened as a form of protection.

Bad days can happen to anyone, there's not much you can do, but you're not alone because millions of people are feeling the same way as you.

Your comeback story will be somebody's inspiration and motivation.

In a world of knives and forks it's alright to be a spoon.

Remember when you thought you couldn't do it, but you did. That's all.

One beautiful day in the future you can look back on any unpleasant present as your past.

Stop worrying about what has happened and asking 'Why?', 'What?', and 'How?'; start focusing on yourself and where you are right now.

You have not been beaten. You are still here.

In the universe there is only one of you, be proud of who you are and what you do.

No matter what you think and how you feel, yes, you matter and yes, you deserve to heal.

Everybody's success is different, it's not just about material wealth; wherever you are on your journey, you should be proud of yourself.

The beautiful thing about imagination is it has no limitations. You should use yours as much as you can and whenever you want.

You can only be in one place at one time so be where you are right now.

If you're exhausted from jumping over hurdles, trying to move mountains, hitting brick walls and picking yourself up after each fall, just breathe and relax, be still and do nothing at all.

You can't go back to the start, but you can make a new beginning; by the time you get to the end you will be singing when you're winning.

No one is going to value you more than you value yourself. Treat yourself like you're worth it because you most certainly are.

In life there are lessons we can learn and things we need to know, like when to hold on, when to give up and when to let go.

Things may seem to be going wrong, but hold on; it might not be tomorrow, but a better day will come along.

This is your life story, it's up to you how quickly you turn the page.

Every time you get knocked down you will get closer to discovering who you really are. You may not feel like it at the moment, but you are awesome.

Listen to what your soul is telling you if it's telling you to rest and recharge.

Storms don't discriminate between race, gender, age, religion and class, but every storm will eventually pass.

Save some energy, switch off negativity, recharge your battery.

Mental health and physical health are just as important as each other; both of them need looking after and both of them can take time to recover.

During the darkness you will shine like a star, you are brighter than you think you are.

Problems will always need solving, but problems won't stop your world from revolving.

Nothing is more exhausting than battling with your own mind every day, it can be so exhausting trying to keep the negative thoughts at bay.

Sending Love To Those . . .

Sending love to those **who struggle to get off the toilet or to get out of bed,**

Sending love to those **with problems with weight loss or weight gain;**

Sending love to those **who lack energy and motivation or frequently need to sit down,**

Sending love to those **who feel like they are going insane.**

Sending love to those **who feel afflicted with addictions,**

Sending love to those **with stress, depression, low moods, phobias and fears;**

Sending love to those **who struggle with the symptoms of their conditions,**

Sending love to those **who want to give up and break down in tears.**

Sending love to those **who are hyperactive, overactive or under active,**

Sending love to those **who feel dizziness, faint or on the verge of collapse;**

Sending love to those **who feel pains, aches, strains and sprains all over their body,**

Sending love to those **who are recovering from suffering or having a relapse.**

Sending love to those **who feel hopeless, helpless, nervous, restless and anxious,**

Sending love to those **who feel tense or an impending sense of danger and doom;**

Sending love to those **who find socialising a nightmare and feel awkward in situations,**

Sending love to those **who feel like they don't belong and unwelcome in any room.**

Sending love to those **with muscle spasms and random uncontrolled movements,**

Sending love to those **who shake, tremble, fidget, tic, droop, flop or jerk;**

Sending love to those **who have problems with reading, writing or numbers,**

Sending love to those **who find it difficult learning new things or getting on with work.**

Sending love to those **who feel they have been a victim of some sort of 'ism,**

Sending love to those **with any kind of syndrome, disorder, dysfunction or disease;**

Sending love to those **who have been lied to, left broken-hearted or cheated on,**

Sending Love To Those . . .

Sending love to those with disturbances, intolerances, deficiencies or allergies.

Sending love to those *who have issues with their body, looks or appearance,*

Sending love to those *who feel blighted by cellulite, dryness or stretch marks on skin;*

Sending love to those *with acne, spots, scars, burns, warts, blemishes or rashes,*

Sending love to those *who wonder when the healing of their sores will begin.*

Sending love to those *who dread and detest examinations or tests,*

Sending love to those *who need replacements, surgery or parts taken away;*

Sending love to those *who feel atrocious from a prognosis or a diagnosis,*

Sending love to those *shrouded in darkness trying to find the lightness of day.*

Sending love to those *who need the volume louder or to hold things closer,*

Sending love to those *who feel chronic from an illness, pain or fatigue;*

Sending love to those *missing a limb, missing the past, missing out, or missing home,*

Sending love to those *who anticipate being relegated at the bottom of the league.*

Sending love to those *dealing with any kind of physical, mental or emotional loss,*

Sending love to those **with heart problems or finding it hard work breathing;**

Sending love to those **with eating disorders or swallowing and choking problems,**

Sending love to those **missing loved ones in moments of reflection and grieving.**

Sending love to those **who find coordination and balance a serious challenge,**

Sending love to those **with restricted movements and problems standing or walking;**

Sending love to those **who feel pains in their heads, shoulders, knees and toes,**

Sending love to those **who have troubles with seeing, hearing, feeling or talking.**

Sending love to those **who feel drowsy, dull, heavy, exhausted, weak or lethargic,**

Sending love to those **with aching tendons, joints, muscles or inflammation;**

Sending love to those **having issues with pressure, digestion, cholesterol or blood,**

Sending love to those **with problems urinating or with vomiting, diarrhoea or constipation.**

Sending Love To Those . . .

Sending love to those *who feel bullied, invisible, haunted or abused,*

Sending love to those *who can't get pregnant or feel empty inside from infertility;*

Sending love to those *with any kind of blindness, deafness, or seizures,*

Sending love to those *who look in the mirror and don't like the reflection they see,*

Sending love to those *who suffer with bad periods or are going through changes,*

Sending love to those *who feel that they can't be themselves;*

Sending love to those *who have no family and friends to rely on,*

Sending love to those *who feel neglected by love or left upon shelves.*

Sending love to those *fed up with medication, therapy and check ups,*

Sending love to those *who have troubles waking up or sleeping at night;*

Sending love to those *who don't feel good enough or hate responsibilities,*

Sending love to those *who feel sick, feverish, sensitive, irregular or not quite right.*

Sending love to those *experiencing memory loss or confusion,*

Sending love to those *who find life tough or struggle financially to get by;*

Sending love to those **who feel lonely, self harmful or have intrusive thoughts,**

Sending love to those **who don't like who or where they are, but don't know why.**

Sending love to those **with conditions ending with itis, itus, ia, ea, ina, ida, es and ma,**

Sending love to those **with conditions ending with ity, ism, iv, sis, epsy and ory too;**

Sending love to those **with conditions ending with pathy, ophy, go, sy, tica and ness,**

Sending love to those **with disabilities, failures or losses that make them feel blue.**

Sending love to those **who are happy with who and how they are,**

Sending love to those **who feel their presence in this world wouldn't be missed;**

Sending love to those **going through hard times, losing hope and trying to cope,**

Sending love to those **who don't see themselves or what they have in a poem or list.**

Bad days

We all have bad days – maybe today was one of them – but having a bad day doesn't mean it has to be a bad life. You've survived your bad days and your worst day, and you are still here. So am I.

My bad days range from losing loved ones and break-ups to injuries and even things like losing a ticket, or saying something silly in a job interview that I regretted. Those types of bad days are quickly forgotten though, or prove to not be as big a deal as they seemed at the time. However, if you let them linger, they can become ingrained in your brain and affect you going forwards, creating more bad days. So it's important to look at your bad days and see them from a different perspective; try and resolve them so you can move on. The fact you survived them and are still here shows you have a hope and desire to do that.

If you can turn your bad days into good lessons and use them in your favour, you can make today a good day – and tomorrow too – and you'll find that soon you're getting a lot more good days than bad ones.

I'm forever trying to do this. It's not easy and I often stumble as I climb this tricky pile of bad lessons and scars from painful moments in my past, but I know that at the top is a view worth going for.

HAPPINESS
ON THE
HORIZON

YOU CAN FEEL HAPPY AGAIN,
IT MIGHT HAVE BEEN A WHILE SINCE YOU FELT LIKE SMILING;
DURING THE SADNESS IT SEEMS LIKE MADNESS TO COMPREHEND
THAT THE MISERY WILL END,
BUT IT WILL MY FRIEND.
BE PROUD THAT YOU'RE FURTHER AWAY FROM THE BEGINNING,
WHEN THE LIGHT AT THE END OF THE TUNNEL LOOKED LIKE A
LIFETIME AWAY
AND YOU NEVER DARED TO DREAM
THAT THERE WOULD BE BATTLES THAT YOU COULD BE WINNING.
EVEN THOUGH THE BURDENS OF RESPONSIBILITIES CAN BE HEAVY
AND MIGHT WEIGH YOU DOWN,
YOU MAY FEEL LIKE A STRANGER WITHOUT A PASSPORT IN YOUR
HOME TOWN,
LOST WITHOUT SIGNS AND DIRECTIONS,
ON CLOSER INSPECTION YOUR REFLECTION SEEMS RESIGNED
TO REJECTION
AND MADE OF STONE;
HOLD ON, BECAUSE THERE WILL BE HAPPINESS ON THE HORIZON
AND YOU WON'T BE ALONE.

You're Incredible
Yes, You Are

NO MATTER WHAT YOU THINK OR HOW YOU FEEL,
YES, YOU MATTER AND YOU NEED TIME TO HEAL;
YOUR MENTAL HEALTH IS A PRIORITY,
YOUR WELL-BEING IS ESSENTIAL
AND YOUR SELF-CARE IS A NECESSITY.
NOBODY REALLY SEES WHAT YOU GO THROUGH
OR HOW YOU DEAL WITH YOUR CONDITION;
YOU TRULY DESERVE HAPPINESS IN YOUR HEART,
THE ACCOLADE OF PRAISE AND RECOGNITION.
YOU ARE WORTHY OF LOVE AND RESPECT,
PLEASE KNOW THAT YOU'RE GOOD ENOUGH;
IT'S OKAY FOR YOU TO SAY NO
AND TO REST WHEN YOU FEEL OVERWHELMED,
ALWAYS ASK FOR HELP IF YOU'RE FINDING THINGS TOUGH.
YOU MIGHT NOT BE INVINCIBLE,
BUT YOU ARE NOT INVISIBLE,
SOME THINGS ARE IMPROBABLE,
BUT THEY ARE NOT IMPOSSIBLE
BECAUSE YOU'RE INCREDIBLE.
YES, YOU ARE.

I MISS YOU SO MUCH

You are the brightest star that shines in the night sky,
You fly with other angels in paradise,
I will love you for eternity; it's only time that
keeps us apart;
Heaven is your home where you feel no pain
and have no fear,
You will be forever missed, I wish you were still here,
But you will always be with me in my mind and
in my heart.
As a way of honouring you I will carry on living my
life and I will get through,
Just like you would want me to do.
There is no wrong or right way to grieve,
I can cry in private or wear my heart on my sleeve;
Some days I'm okay and some days I get sad,
Sometimes I'm a blubbering mess, but I feel blessed
for the time that we had.
You brightened up my world while you were here
on Earth,
And even though I sometimes cry;
I'm so glad that we had each other,
Our love is eternal and will never die.
I promise I will never forget you;
I will find my smile again one day;
I will love you forever
And the memories will never fade away.

What if?

What if the worst happens? What if I lose my job? What if I go crazy? What if I can't find love? What if I die? (Spoiler alert. You will die one day. All of us will die one day. That's life… and death. There's no need to be afraid. In all of the 'what if' scenarios, it's the only 'what if' that's certain. There's no need to fear what's for certain. It will be alright.)

I often play out every worst-case scenario in my head when I'm stressed, and it sends me down an absolute rabbit hole of worry. And there's no cute bunny rabbits to chat to either. But it's something that I've stopped doing as much.

Here is an example of how it would go:

Me: Ohhhhh, I feel a bit weird. Is that a tingling sensation in my arm? Yes. It definitely is. Am I having a stroke? Hold on a minute. I can feel tightness in my chest. I'm sure I'm having a heart attack. What if I'm having a heart attack? Will any of these people around me know how to save me if I am? I wonder if they have trained in first aid and know how to do CPR? Oh my god, I'm definitely going to collapse. I've not collapsed yet, but it's going to happen. Or maybe it won't. I think I'm dying. I'm definitely going to die. What will my family do without me? Will my wife be made homeless and not be able to afford to pay bills?

Will she be alone for the rest of her life? How many people will turn up at my funeral? I'm not that popular. Why haven't I got many friends? Is there something wrong with me? There must be. Will I be missed? I don't want people to be too upset if I die. Will my death break my family apart? What do I do? What will they do?

And so on and so on and so on. But every bad time that I have had, I have got through. And you have too. The majority of what ifs and worst-case scenarios don't actually end up coming true and if they do, we will get through them. What if what you're worrying about doesn't happen and what if something marvellous happens instead?

A Boomerang That Doesn't Work Is Just A Stick

Incorrectly is spelled incorrectly in the dictionary,
If you go browsing at a boat shop there are always sails;
Oysters never donate to charity because they are shellfish,
Fish are easy to weigh because they have their own scales.
A witch won't wear a flat cap because there's no point in it,
The house went to the doctor because it had window pane;
The strongest bird in the world is most definitely the crane.
The party on the moon was rubbish because it had no atmosphere,
You can find an ocean without water on any map;
Build a bar on the roof and the drinks are always on the house,
Take a ruler or a measuring tape to bed to see how long you nap.
Traffic jam can not be eaten on toast;
The banker was bored when he lost interest in everything,
Lies can be disguised, but it's easy to see through any ghost.
Horses that go out when it's dark are nightmares,
Tubes of glue are loyal because they always stick together;
Angels greet each other by saying 'halo',
An octopus may wear a coat of many arms in the winter weather.
Prisoners in jail might communicate by using cell phones,
Two skunks arguing may kick up a stink;
A fly without wings could just be called a walk,
Root beer is a tree's most favourite drink.
Tooth-hurty is the best time to see a dentist,
When magicians go on holiday they never miss a trick;
A vegetable may need a plumber if it's a leek,
A boomerang that doesn't work is just a stick.

HELLO YOU.
JUST LIKE ME, IT'S IMPOSSIBLE FOR YOU TO
ALWAYS FEEL SUPER OR FULL.
IF YOU'RE FEELING BLUE, PLEASE KNOW IT'S JUST
A PHASE.
THERE WILL BE TIMES WHEN IT SEEMS LIKE THERE IS NO
ATMOSPHERE WHEREVER YOU GO, AND YOU JUST NEED
YOUR OWN SPACE. THAT'S OKAY.
WE ALL HAVE A DARK SIDE AND IT WOULD BE LUNAR
SEA TO THINK THAT WE CAN SHINE BRIGHT ALL OF
THE TIME.
WHEN WE ARE SURROUNDED BY DARKNESS THE STARS
AROUND US EMERGE AND HELP MAKE THINGS LIGHTER.
EVEN IF THE GRAVITY BRINGS YOU DOWN IT WON'T
ECLIPSE HOW GREAT YOU ARE OR THE SMALL STEPS AND
GIANT LEAPS YOU CAN MAKE.
SLEEP WELL AND HAVE WONDERFUL DREAMS.
IF YOU CAN'T SLEEP, JUST DO SOMETHING YOU ENJOY
DOING INSTEAD (AS LONG AS IT'S NOT TOO NOISY) AND
LOOK OUT OF THE WINDOW OCCASIONALLY AND SAY
HELLO TO ME.
I WILL BE HERE EVERY NIGHT UNTIL THE SUN COMES UP.
LOVE YOU LOADS.

IF YOU'RE RUNNING OUT OF SPACE
TO SWEEP YOUR PROBLEMS
UNDER A CARPET OR A RUG;
IF YOU THINK
YOUR GLASS OR CUP IS
HALF EMPTY AND THAT
YOU GET TREATED LIKE A MUG;
IF YOU'RE A BUSY BEE
LONGING TO FLOAT
LIKE A BUTTERFLY,
BUT YOU FEEL BUGGED AND
MORE LIKE A SLUG;
IF YOU'RE TIRED FROM
UNTANGLING CROSSED WIRES
UNTIL SOMEONE PULLS THE PLUG;
IF YOU FEEL THIS WAY,
WE ARE SENDING YOU
A VIRTUAL HUG.

EVEN THE SUN CAN FEEL
UNDER THE WEATHER,
EVEN A SCIENTIST MAY NOT
FEEL SO CLEVER;
EVEN AN ALARM CLOCK
MAY JUST WANT TO SNOOZE,
EVEN A WINNER KNOWS
WHAT IT FEELS LIKE TO LOSE.
EVEN A DANCER MAY NOT
BE IN THE GROOVE,
EVEN A CHESS PIECE MAY
NOT WANT TO MOVE;
EVEN A SINGER CAN
SOUND OUT OF TUNE,
EVEN THE MONTH OF APRIL
MAY JUST WANT TO BE JUNE;
EVEN AN EXPLORER CAN BE
LOST IN A MAZE,
EVERYONE AND EVERYTHING
CAN HAVE BAD DAYS.

Money

Money can't buy love or happiness, but it can certainly cheer us up a bit. So many worries and arguments are caused because of money, normally due to a lack of it.

If you have ever played the board game Monopoly, I can guarantee that at some point someone has said, 'If only this was real money,' when looking down at all of the Monopoly cash.

There's that saying that goes 'money is the root of all evil', but then it all depends on who's holding the money and where that money is going. If given the choice to be happy but poor or miserable but rich, I would choose the happiness option all the time. Then I would get the rich person's address and ask them to lend us some money. It would be rude not to.

BORN
TO BE
MILD

WISTFULLY WONDERING AND WANDERING,
RELAXING WHILE PEACEFULLY PONDERING;
THE RELIEF FROM DEEP BREATHING AND UNTANGLING CROSSED WIRES
FEELS LIKE LOOSENING TROUSERS OR UNDOING A TIE.
QUIETLY SILENCING A RIOT IN THE BRAIN
LIKE A LIBRARY ON A SUMMER SUNDAY AFTERNOON;
LIKE THE SERENITY OF A MIDNIGHT STREAM
HOLDING THE REFLECTION OF THE MOON.
UNFIXING WASTED FIXATIONS ON SITUATIONS
THAT WERE NEVER MEANT TO BE;
PATIENTLY ANTICIPATING FRUSTRATIONS BEING WASHED AWAY
BY SAVING WAVES OF TRANQUILITY.
A CAREFREE MIND GLIDING LIKE A BALLERINA
PERFORMING MESMERISING PIROUETTES;
AT EASE IN THE GENTLE BREEZE
AND DANCING FREELY WITH JOY AND POSSIBILITIES
LIKE A HELIUM BALLOON,
ESCAPING REALITY REASSURED BY A SAFETY NET.
SOOTHED BY THE GROOVES OF SMOOTH MUSIC
AND THE MOVEMENT OF PLAYFUL SILHOUETTES.
IN TUNE WITH THE RHYTHMIC MELODY
OF AN EXPERIMENTAL INSTRUMENTAL
FROM THE RAIN ON A WINDOW PANE.
SAFE AND LOVED LIKE A TEDDY BEAR OR A SOFT TOY
BEING CUDDLED BY THE ARMS OF A CHILD;
COMFORTABLE IN COSY, FURRY SLIPPERS
THAT ADD TWINKLES TO TOES
OR FEELING ROSY IN A FRESH NEW PAIR OF SOCKS WITH NO HOLES,
WHILE THE WHISTLING WIND WHISPERS MOTHER NATURE'S
INSTRUCTIONS
TO REST STILL AND BE MILD.

CARING
FOR
YOURSELF

Caring for yourself
Isn't always about eating healthy, exercising
Or having an early night;
It can be admitting to others that you're not okay
Or there's something wrong
When someone asks you if you're alright.
Don't leave it too late
And always pay attention
To what your body and mind are trying to say;
Nobody is too young, too old, too healthy
or too pretty
to experience issues with their health and their
mental health today.
When your body and mind start talking
It's time to start listening,
They could be telling you that you need some help
Or that you need to rest;
Be attentive to them
Just like you would want a good friend to be
attentive to you,
Doing what's right for you is always for the best.

DEAR FUTURE SELF

DEAR FUTURE SELF,

HOPE YOU'RE DOING OKAY?
WHEREVER YOU ARE AND WHATEVER YOU'RE DOING;
I'M SORRY I LOST MY WAY SOMETIMES ON THE ROAD TO RECOVERY
AND ALMOST ENDED UP ON A ROAD TO RUIN.
THERE ARE DAYS WHEN I STRUGGLE AND AT TIMES LIFE GETS HARD,
BUT FOR THE BENEFIT OF YOU AND ME
I WON'T GIVE IN;
SOME PEOPLE SAY LIFE IS A GAME
AND IT SEEMS EVEN WHEN I FOLLOW THE RULES,
I LOSE MORE THAN I WIN.
I NEED TO BE KIND TO MYSELF
AND LOOK AFTER MYSELF BETTER,
FOR YOU I WANT TO TRULY DO MY BEST;
YOU AND I DESERVE TO BE
IN A MUCH BETTER PLACE
WITH A BETTER STATE OF MIND,
INSTEAD OF BEING IN A STATE OF EXHAUSTION
AND STRESSED.
HOW LONG DID THE LIGHT AT THE END OF THE TUNNEL TAKE TO ARRIVE?
DID I LEARN FROM THE EXPERIENCES OF ALL THE MISTAKES I MADE
DURING THIS PRESENT TIME?
AFTER THINKING I COULDN'T COPE AM I HAPPIER IN THE FUTURE?
DID I REACH THE TOP OF THE MOUNTAIN OF HOPE THAT I WAS
DESPERATE TO CLIMB?

TAKE CARE,
LOVE, ME

Emerge Like A Butterfly
From A Cocoon

Instead of being weighed down by unrealistic expectations in isolation
and fed up with frustration,
You can spend time working on your transformation;
By all means keep being you,
But think about things to do
that can help to improve your situation;
Before you know it you will be excited
and delighted by anticipation.
Maybe not today or tomorrow,
but the better days will be coming soon,
When you will be shining like the stars
and floating over the moon;
There will be days when the sun doesn't want to play,
but that's okay,
In a world of knives and forks, it's alright to be a spoon;
Every caterpillar becomes a butterfly,
and one day you will emerge from your cocoon.

Forget The Regrets Of The Past

Forget the regrets of the past
and the bridges you never crossed;
Don't lose any sleep about missed
opportunities
and what they may have cost;
It's time to stop dwelling on the wars
you won
and the battles you think you lost.
Focus on the present and where you
are right now,
Try to find some positivity in every day;
At times it may seem like you're in a long
term relationship with sadness or grief,
A healing process can be slow and as if
there's no relief,
Hold on to yourself and eventually you
will find your way.

HONOURING
<u>YOU</u>

YOU MAY NOT EVER BE GIVEN A KNIGHTHOOD,

YOU MAY NOT EVER BE MADE A DAME;

YOU MAY NOT EVER BE INCLUDED ON A

NEW YEAR'S HONOURS LIST

AND GIVEN LETTERS TO PUT AFTER YOUR NAME.

YOU MAY NOT ALWAYS BE GIVEN CREDIT OR PRAISE,

YOU MAY NOT GET THE RECOGNITION FOR WHAT YOU DO;

YOU TRULY DESERVE HAPPINESS

AND ALL OF THE GOOD THINGS IN LIFE,

PLEASE SEE THIS MESSAGE AS A WAY OF HONOURING YOU.

YES, <u>YOU</u>.
THANKS FOR BEING <u>YOU</u>.

I AM THE SURVIVOR

UNDERGROUND

It's hard to manage when I'm feeling damaged,
If ever that happens I need to challenge my past;
Whatever I went through I survived
And made it through to the other side,
I'm still alive,
and between me and the trauma
who is the one left standing last?
Traumatic events in the past can cause torment,
But I am not suffering in that time and place right now;
For whatever reason what happened happened to me,
But I got through it and there's no need for me to keep
on questioning myself with 'Why?' or 'How?'.
I can be bigger than the triggers
causing me negative symptoms,
I will pick myself up if they knock me to the ground;
There are times when I'm unkindly reminded
of traumas and tragic events
by bad news, or hearing a certain sound;
What happened once before may have shocked me
and rocked me to the core,
But that moment no longer exists,
I am the survivor
who stayed strong and stuck around.

I DON'T WANT TO
FEEL FRUSTRATED,
I WANT TO
FEEL APPRECIATED;
I DON'T WANT TO
FEEL LONELY,
I WANT TO FEEL LIKE
THE ONE AND ONLY;
I DON'T WANT TO
FEEL INVISIBLE,
I WANT TO
FEEL INCREDIBLE;
I DON'T WANT TO
FEEL LIKE I JUST EXIST,
I WANT TO FEEL LIKE
I WOULD BE MISSED.

I'm Not The Only Lonely One

Loneliness makes me feel like a ghost being
haunted by myself;
Abandoned like an unexpected item in a bagging area
or past it's sell-by date,
left on the supermarket shelf.
Loneliness finds my thoughts pondering
and then I'm wandering off the beaten track;
It seems at times I've been rejected with
no connections
or given no directions to find my way back.
Loneliness leaves me believing
I'm an outcast surrounded by a crowd;
It stretches out the hours of the day
and turns up the volume of a silent night too loud.
Loneliness imprisons me with invisible chains
as my shoelaces come undone;
But every honest conversation
can improve my situation
and show me I'm not the only lonely one.

A GOOD NIGHT'S SLEEP

I OFTEN DREAM OF A GOOD NIGHT'S SLEEP
ONE THAT HELPS ME TO RECOVER
AND IS UNINTERRUPTED AND DEEP;
A HEALING PERIOD OF TIME THAT'S A RESPITE
FROM ME BEING STRESSED,
AN EIGHT HOUR SLUMBER THAT RECHARGES MY BATTERY
AND PROVIDES ME WITH SUFFICIENT REST.
MY DREAMS SPEAK TO ME WHEN I'M DEEP IN SLUMBER,
I'M NOT SURE WHAT THEY ARE TRYING TO SAY;
SOME OF THEM I FORGET AS SOON AS I WAKE UP
IN THE MORNING AND WONDER,
SOME DREAMS I REMEMBER FOR THE REST OF THE DAY.
MAYBE I WON'T EVER BE AWARDED FOR BEING KIND,
BUT, IF I'M REWARDED WITH A GOOD NIGHT'S SLEEP
AND PEACE OF MIND,
I CERTAINLY DON'T MIND.

UNDERGROUND

I NEED TO LET GO
OF THINKING ABOUT PEOPLE
WHO ARE UNSUPPORTIVE
AND DON'T THINK ABOUT ME;
I NEED TO LET GO
OF ALWAYS TRYING TO BE IN CONTROL
AND LEARN HOW TO LET THINGS BE.
I NEED TO LET GO
OF COMPARING MY LIFE
AND MY DRAMAS TO OTHERS
AND TRYING TO
LIVE UP TO UNREALISTIC EXPECTATIONS;
I NEED TO LET GO
OF FEARING FAILURE,
HANGING ON TO FEELINGS
THAT EAT ME ALIVE AND WORRYING
ABOUT BAD SITUATIONS.
I NEED TO LET GO
OF SO MANY THINGS THAT MAKE IT
DIFFICULT FOR ME TO COPE;
I NEED TO LET GO
OF THE THINGS DOING ME DAMAGE,
SO I CAN GET A HOLD OF MYSELF
AND HOLD ON TO HOPE.

Dreams

As an insomniac and someone who has issues with sleep in general, dreams are something I rarely, if at all, experience anymore. I've found myself begging to have a nightmare just because it would mean I've got some deep sleep.

Dreams are wonderful, especially when they feel so real that you are completely convinced you can fly or do impossible things and go to fantastical places. When they are that amazing, or when they have people in them you deeply miss, it's sad to wake up and realise it's not real. Some dreams deserve to be real but, like everything in life, they don't last forever, so when you have those wonderful moments make sure you hold them in your heart as much as you would any beautiful real-life experience and remember the happiness they brought you.

You never know when you may get to dream again.

IF SLEEPING IS A BETTER REALITY
FOR YOU THAN REAL LIFE
AND EVERY DAY SEEMS LIKE YOU
WAKE UP INTO A NIGHTMARE,
CHANGES DESPERATELY NEED TO
BE MADE;
IF YOU'VE STARTED TO THINK THAT
LIVING IS HARDER THAN DYING,
THE TIME FOR YOU TO GET HELP IS
RIGHT NOW
AND SHOULDN'T BE DELAYED.

INSOMNIA

I really need to sleep, but my mind decides to replay
every decision I've ever made,
It feels like I'm the only person awake at three in the morning;
If sleep is a punchline to a joke, I never seem to get it,
In my head I hear voices chatting instead of lullabies,
Even the sheep I've tried counting are tired and yawning.
Insomnia is stopping me from dreaming
And has put me in a nightmare,
An army of noisy flies and mosquitoes are buzzing in my brain;
It's a vicious circle when the best cure for insomnia is getting
plenty of sleep,
I'm a heavy cloud in need of desperate relief
and refusing to rain.
It's a test being restless, it's a long night of loneliness,
Having the company of the TV, the Internet, the radio
or a book to read;
I'm wide awake in bed,
Evicted from my dreams and doing something else instead,
Staring at the ceiling and worrying about how many hours sleep
I really need.
Ironically, I try not to lose any sleep over insomnia,
But, for goodness sake, why does it keep me awake?
I'm not in the land of the living or the land of nod,
I'm stuck somewhere in between;
Getting up in the morning is something my heavy eyelids dread,
I know I will be strolling like the walking dead,
If insomnia kept me awake when I needed it to
I would save so much money that I spend on caffeine.

IT ISN'T RIGHT

IT ISN'T RIGHT
THAT 9 TIMES OUT OF 10
I WAKE UP ON THE WRONG SIDE OF BED;
IT ISN'T RIGHT
THAT I'M ALWAYS BATTLING WITH DEMONS IN MY HEAD.
IT ISN'T RIGHT
THAT I TRIED TO DISGUISE MY SADNESS
BY WEARING A FAKE SMILE;
IT ISN'T RIGHT
THAT I FEEL LIKE I DON'T DESERVE HAPPINESS
AND ALWAYS QUESTION IF I'M WORTHWHILE;
IT ISN'T RIGHT
THAT I DON'T COUNT MY BLESSINGS
BECAUSE I FEEL LIKE I'M CURSED;
IT ISN'T RIGHT
WHEN I PICTURE SCENARIOS
I ALWAYS SEE THE WORST.
IT ISN'T RIGHT
THAT EVERY DAY SEEMS LIKE A FIGHT
AND A MISSION FOR ME TO SURVIVE;
IT ISN'T RIGHT
THAT I FEEL LIKE I'M JUST EXISTING
INSTEAD OF FEELING ALIVE

It's Okay To Be You
And It's Okay To Be Me

Everyone we meet is fighting a battle that can't be seen,
Just because others may not see
it doesn't mean that it's not there;
It's not your fault for having negative thoughts,
But there are reasons for you being alive,
The weight of the world is lessened with every lesson we
learn and share.
Your life shouldn't conform because of fears,
Of being ostracised for being different
Or threatened and ignored by your peers,
Nudged towards the brink of non-existence
and feeling lost at sea;
You are special and you are worthwhile,
You may not feel like doing it,
But the world lights up when you smile,
Please know that it's okay to be you and its okay to be me.

Letting go

There are times when you need to hold on to things and there are times when you need to let go. Sometimes you have to let go to be able to hold on.

It would be amazing if our troubles, worries, fear, anxieties and sadness were helium balloons and we could just let go of them and watch them float away. Over time we can do that, but unfortunately they are not as easy to let go of as balloons are. If your hands are full trying to carry the weight of the world, or you're juggling too many things, you need to share the burden with someone.

When I was a train driver and a girl jumped in front of my train, I experienced Post-Traumatic Stress Disorder and had a really tough time driving trains. It got to the point where I had to let go of my train driving career in order to hold on to the well-being of my mental health. I would choose to be happy (or at least happier) over money any day of the week.

Hold on to people you love, hold on to the things that matter the most, and always hold on to hope. If you're going through tough times and you're in a dark place, please hold on, because there will be better and brighter days.

Loneliness

If you are reading this and you feel lonely, we are sending so much love to you.

The feeling of loneliness can happen to anyone at any time, and it's obviously not a nice feeling.

You can feel lonely if you are on your own and have no family or friends to turn to.

You can feel lonely in relationships, when a loved one or a pet has passed away, or if you are dealing with issues and feel like you are the only one in the world to be going through something.

You can even feel lonely when surrounded by many other people. The London Underground is one of the busiest places in the world and yet it can feel like one of the loneliest places too.

The three years after I left school were, without a doubt, the loneliest. I experienced depression and even medication didn't improve things for long. My friends had moved to universities far away, but in order to get through university financially I lived at home, so I didn't merge with university life and struggled to make new friends there. I found myself going to and from classes in almost complete silence and continuing this trend at home. I did very little of anything. It was a spiral, a deep and cold one, and it's the cold of it that makes loneliness so hard to endure.

People can give us warmth the sun cannot compete with, and yet I was often in the midst of people and still never felt that warmth. It took years for things to improve and I can still remember every corner of a packed room where I once hid, and can remember how it felt. I know that I could go to those same places today and recognise that same feeling, but also the far better reality of my life now.

I can't say I have a magic answer that will get you through loneliness but I can say that I got through it so you can too.

ONE NEGATIVE COMMENT

WHY CAN ONE NEGATIVE COMMENT SOMETIMES
RUIN YOUR DAY?
IN YOUR MIND YOU KEEP ANALYSING IT
AND THINKING OF CLEVER REPLIES EACH TIME
YOU PRESS REWIND AND PLAY;
TRY TO FORGET ABOUT IT AND FOCUS ON ALL OF
THE POSITIVE THINGS IN YOUR LIFE
AND ACCEPT ANY COMPLIMENTS THAT MIGHT
COME YOUR WAY.
PEOPLE TREAT YOU THE WAY THEY FEEL ABOUT YOU,
THEIR WORDS MAY SAY SOMETHING ELSE,
BUT THEIR BEHAVIOUR AND THEIR ACTIONS CAN'T
ALWAYS LIE;
EVEN WHEN SOMEBODY GETS COMFORTABLE
WITH YOU
THEY SHOULDN'T TAKE ADVANTAGE OR LOSE
APPRECIATION OF HOW SPECIAL YOU ARE,
IF THEY DO IT ONCE TOO OFTEN
THEN IT'S TIME FOR YOU TO START TALKING
OR START THINKING OF SAYING GOODBYE.

Recovery (Your Comeback Story)

There will come a time when you can't
sink any further
And it seems like you can never win;
The moment you realise that you've
reached your lowest point
Is the moment when your recovery will
start to begin.
At the moment you may be struggling
in what feels like a no way out
desperate situation;
But you will get through it and in
the future your comeback story
and recovery
will be somebody's inspiration and
motivation.

SPACE

HUMANKIND'S FASCINATION WITH SPACE STATIONS AND EXPLORATION
CAN HELP UNITE NATIONS AND DISCOVER WHAT IS TRUE;
FROM THE BIG BANG THEORY TO A SATELLITE'S PERSISTENCE,
ARE WE ALONE SEARCHING FOR THE MEANING OF EXISTENCE?
IT'S INCONCEIVABLE TO BELIEVE THE OCEANS OF EARTH ARE NOTHIN' BUT BLUE.
THE MAN ON THE MOON IS AN INTERSTELLAR FELLA
AND THROUGH THE VOID OF SPACE HE HAS CONTACT WITH A GIRL FROM MARS;
THE SERENITY OF ZERO GRAVITY MADE E.T PHONE HOME,
WE SHARE THE BIG DREAM TO SPACE TRAVEL AS WE LOOK TO THE STARS
ANY SPACE ODYSSEY CAN BE A SPACE ODDITY ALL ACROSS THE UNIVERSE
FROM THE MYSTERY OF A BLACK HOLE TO THE BEAUTY OF THE MILKY WAY;
A GALAXY AND A CLUSTER OF STARS CAN INSPIRE BLOCKBUSTERS IN CINEMAS,
LIKE DARK MATTER SCATTERED IN THE LYRICS OF THE SONGS WE SING TODAY.
IS THE MOON MADE OF CHEESE?, DO ALIENS LOVE UNDERPANTS?
IS THE UNIVERSE REALLY EXPANDING?
ASTRONAUTS AND SPACE SCIENTISTS ON A MISSION
CAN SEPARATE THE FACTS FROM SCIENCE FICTION
AND OPEN OUR MINDS TO GIVE US A BETTER UNDERSTANDING.

STOP/START

STOP SHINING THE SPOTLIGHT
ON YOUR DEFEATS
AND HIGHLIGHTING EVERY SPACE IN YOUR LIFE
THAT'S INCOMPLETE,
STOP FOCUSSING ON REGRETS
AND WHAT YOU ARE NOT;
START CELEBRATING EACH SMALL VICTORY
AND START TO BELIEVE,
START FEELING PROUD WITH WHAT YOU ACHIEVE,
START APPRECIATING HOW FAR YOU'VE COME
AND ALL THE THINGS YOU HAVE GOT.

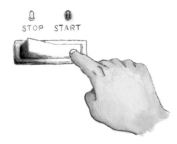

TEARS
ARE LITTLE MESSAGES
OF OVERWHELMING GRIEF,
THAT SPEAK
LOUDER THAN WORDS
AND DESCRIBE
HOW WE ARE
FEELING BENEATH.

What is life all about?

What is the meaning of life? Honestly, I haven't got a clue.

It is completely bonkers when you think about it. We are on a rock the shape of a ball floating in space surrounded by stars and other planets and the universe could potentially go on forever and nobody really knows why.

There's a reason behind everything, but nobody really knows why existence happened. They may be able to tell you how, with the Big Bang theories, the fish growing legs and all that jazz, but nobody knows the reason why.

Some people believe in Heaven and some people don't, believing it's a far-fetched idea and it isn't possible. I totally believe in Heaven. Stranger things have happened since the start of time for me not to believe.

But whatever you believe, we only have one life, unless we believe in reincarnation or are cats showing off with nine lives, so we may as well try to enjoy it.

THE DEMANDS OF LIFE

IT'S HARD TO STAY MOTIVATED WHEN FACED WITH THE
DEMANDS OF LIFE
AND YOU'RE TRYING TO KEEP THE SHARKS, THE VULTURES
AND BARKING DEMON DOGS AT BAY;
WHILE YOU'RE BUSY PLANNING AND SAVING FOR THINGS YOU
WANT NOW AND IN THE FUTURE
UNFORESEEN CIRCUMSTANCES PUT A HOLE IN THE BUCKET OF
YOUR RAINY DAY FUND.
FINANCIAL RESPONSIBILITIES AND WORRIES HAVE AN ANNOYING
HABIT OF GETTING IN THE WAY;
CONSTANT COMMITMENTS CONSISTENTLY SEEM TO PILE UP
AND IT CAN BE A CHALLENGE FINDING THE RIGHT BALANCE
TO MANAGE,
SETTING GOALS, MAKING PLANS AND DOING WHAT YOU
WANT TO DO
CAN LEAVE YOU FEELING FRUSTRATED AT THE END OF THE DAY.
FAILING TO ACHIEVE MIGHT LEAVE YOU QUESTIONING WHAT YOU
ACTUALLY BELIEVE,
BUT DON'T BE DISHEARTENED, TAKE IT ONE STEP AT A TIME;
THE REALISATION THAT YOU NEED HELP
IS A BLESSING IN DISGUISE
AND WILL HELP YOU TO PREPARE FOR THE MOUNTAINS THAT
YOU NEED TO CLIMB.

Some Nights The Morning Comes Too Soon

In the morning I'm tired,
In the afternoon I need to rest,
and yet when it comes to bedtime I can't sleep.
I lay wide awake in the darkness for hours,
Wanting to switch off,
But my brain is thinking of every possible thing;
If the day is a shift
my mind is working overtime at night
and not getting paid,
When I should be relaxing on the bed I made.
During the silence of the night my buzzing
thoughts are deafening
until they get replaced by the sound of the
morning birds and the songs they sing.
I'm tossing and turning as the world is dreaming;
I wish counting sheep could help me sleep,
It's torture when I'm on my own in the twilight zone,
Listening to my brain chattering.
I've forgotten what a normal sleep pattern is,
Some nights the morning comes too soon
and I feel like a zombie by the afternoon,
My restless brain has it in for me,
Keeping me company
when I just want to be left alone.

What will happen tomorrow?

It's a question we all often ask ourselves, but not in the way that maybe we should: what will happen tomorrow? Will my idea for a real hoverboard from *Back to the Future* be given the go ahead? Will I go to the beach and do nothing but enjoy the breeze of the sea and the visions it offers? Will I propose to the love of my life even though I didn't have a plan to?

It's the plan bit that always gets me looking at it the wrong way. What will happen tomorrow? My hoverboard idea will flop because I didn't think of some technical issue. The trains might not be running so I can't get to the beach. My proposal might go wrong because I didn't plan it.

What will happen tomorrow?

The older I get, the more I realise that that question had so much more innocence and magic when I was a child. It's that wonder that I am constantly trying to get back to. It's a question that tests your perspective and the answer you give tells you if you are focusing more on the negatives or the positives of life. Shouldn't we all look forward to tomorrow rather than dreading it?

Maybe that's what will happen tomorrow . . .

The Sunrise Will Greet
You Like A Friend

Rise like the sun,
Today will be whatever you make it;
If you don't wake up with a smile
There's no need to fake it;
Start the day in your own way,
If an opportunity arises and suits you
then take it.
Darkness can sometimes surround you,
Like a night without stars
to light up the skies;
It won't be long until you see the sun rise.
It's easier said than done,
But try to stress less,
You will get through this
And everything will work out in the end;
Hold on, because it will be alright,
You will survive the dramas of the day
and the loneliness of the night,
After the darkness the sunrise will
greet you like a friend.

THERE WILL BE TIMES

There will be times when you feel like the butt of the joke
and as if you're wearing the shoes of a circus clown;
There will be times when you're taken by surprise
and caught with your trousers down.
There will be times of tragedy and anxiety,
Feeling fearful and being scared;
There will be times when you feel overworked,
unappreciated and ill-prepared.

There will be times when your heart gets broken,
At some point everyone will grieve;
There will be times when your dreams seem unreachable
and you think that happy endings are just make-believe.
There will be times when you can't find the answers,
even with a search engine, and so question yourself;
When you feel like your best before date has expired
and that you're undesired and left on the shelf.

There will be times when you feel that everyone else
is having fun at the party of life and you're the
disappointed, uninvited guest;
There will be times when no amount of self-help books and
yoga sessions can prevent you from being stressed.
There will be times of trouble, sadness and madness,
and when your faith seems to buckle
as you're praying on your knees;
Time is temporary and one thing that's certain,
If you're having it rough and finding life tough,
There will be times much better than these.

Sleeping

We all need sleep. It's a necessity for living. How hard can it be? You can sleep in many different places – through a bad movie, on your commute, etc – but in your own bed is the best place, so just put on your PJs, curl up in a bed and job done, right?

Yet for some people it's not so easy. Many people struggle to sleep because of health or world conditions, or both.

I struggle with sleep. A haze or interrupted slouch are the two options I experience most nights and dreams of bliss exist only as an idea rather than a reality. This is because of insomnia and tinnitus, and sometimes both.

Sleep is wonderful when it's good and it really is so important. We should cherish a good night's sleep because it's not promised and you could suddenly find yourself as someone who doesn't really get to sleep the way you once did, which can affect a lot of things.

If you struggle with sleep please know you are not alone, many others do too. It won't be that way forever and, although you may not be able to dream of wonderful days, you can still do what you can to make the time you're awake worthy of dreams.

THERE WILL BE BETTER DAYS AHEAD

THERE WILL BE BETTER DAYS IN THE FUTURE, SO KEEP GOING,
TRY TO STOP WASTING TIME WORRYING IF THINGS WILL BE OKAY;
DON'T LET OTHER PEOPLE'S OPINIONS CHANGE WHO YOU ARE
AND FROM THOSE WHO WALK BESIDE YOU, DON'T RUN AWAY.
BE BRAVE, BE CONFIDENT, BE HONEST AND BE YOU,
DO WHAT MAKES YOU HAPPY, TAKE TIME TO TAKE IT ALL IN
AND ENJOY THE VIEW,
TRY NEW THINGS INSTEAD OF STICKING TO WHAT YOU KNOW;
IGNORE NEGATIVITY
BECAUSE YOU CAN'T CONTROL WHAT OTHERS PERCEIVE,
HAVE FAITH IN YOURSELF AND STICK TO WHAT YOU BELIEVE,
DON'T OVERTHINK WHEN YOU PONDER,
CHERISH MOMENTS THAT SHOULDN'T BE SQUANDERED,
WHEN LIFE SEEMS TO BE GOING TOO FAST,
PULL OVER OR TAKE IT SLOW.
YOU MAY NOT SEE HOW THINGS CAN GET BETTER,
BUT THE SAME DARKNESS THAT IS TELLING YOU THAT YOU
MIGHT BE BETTER OFF DEAD,
IS THE SAME DARKNESS THAT IS HIDING THE LIGHT
AND BLINDING YOU TO THE FACT THAT THERE WILL BE BETTER
DAYS AHEAD.

THINGS

The things I worry about shouldn't really matter,
But at the moment they seem to matter to me;
I don't know where my mind goes wandering
when it's thinking things over,
But I'm sure it's looking for other places to be.
Things may happen beyond my control,
It doesn't mean I can't control how I behave;
I can't control the rough sea from trying to shipwreck me,
But I can learn how to surf and ride every wave.
I want to say 'yes' to things I won't be able to do
when I'm older,
I hope to discover new things on a completely different path;
I should do my own thing and enjoy the things I'm doing,
Embrace who I am and the people and things
that make me laugh.
I need to savour the things that make my life worth living
When it's wearing me down and I'm finding things tough;
I shouldn't overlook simple pleasures,
Every one can create moments to treasure
And each one should be cherished
like a diamond in the rough.
I need to think of things I've always wanted to do
and just do them,
Everything has a new meaning when someone pursues a dream;
I want to reach for things on the horizon
knowing that if I fail things won't be as bad as they seem.

When You're Good And Ready

You don't need to explain who you are and your pain
or the negative thoughts in your brain;
You are not alone in questioning and thinking
to yourself,
'Is it me or is it the rest of the world that's
going insane?'
Give it time and you will find your smile again.
Try to let go of your worries
and stop trying to control what can't be controlled;
Some people look so self-assured,
But nobody really knows what life is all about.
Give yourself space to relax and breathe,
It's you that sets the limit to what you can achieve,
So believe in yourself and have faith that things will
eventually work out.
Take time for yourself,
Do things that bring joy to your heart;
If there are hurdles in your path they can all be
jumped over,
When you're good and ready to carry on
or to make a brand new start.

WOMEN
SHOULD FEEL
SAFE

WOMEN SHOULDN'T HAVE TO BE CAREFUL WITH WHAT THEY WEAR,
WALK HOME SCARED, GRIP THEIR KEYS IN THEIR HAND
AS THEY WANDER HOME, BE TOLD TO STAY IN GROUPS
AND NOT TO GO OUT AT NIGHT;
WOMEN SHOULDN'T HAVE TO BE TAUGHT SAFETY PRECAUTIONS,
CARRY PERSONAL ALARMS, BE ADVISED TO LOOK OVER THEIR SHOULDERS,
STARTLED BY FOOTSTEPS FROM BEHIND, WALK FACING ONCOMING TRAFFIC,
FEEL THE NEED TO DOUBLE BACK OR SEND TEXTS SAYING
'BE SAFE', 'TEXT ME WHEN YOU GET HOME' AND 'TAKE EXTRA CARE';
WOMEN SHOULDN'T HAVE TO TAKE LONGER ROUTES,
BE SCRAED OF BUSHES AND SHADOWS, NOT WEAR EARPHONES,
MAKE FAKE PHONE CALLS, BE HYPER VIGILANT OF ASSAULT
OR BE TAUGHT HOW TO DEFEND THEMSELVES JUST IN CASE;
WE NEED TO GET TO THE ROOT OF THE PROBLEM,
WE NEED TO LEARN AND CHANGE CERTAIN BEHAVIOURS,
WE NEED TO MAKE WOMEN FEEL SAFE EVERYWHERE.

Finding peace

For me life is about peace and finding it as much as possible, whether that be within myself, with who I am or with the world. I genuinely believe that we all have a purpose to make this world a peaceful place for those here now and those who inherit it after we're gone.

Peace can be found in many places – from sailing on a boat in calm waters to lying on a sunny beach, from the moment anxiety is lifted from your shoulders, in the embrace of loved ones or even in the warmth of a cup of tea – but at its core is harmony, and surely the world would be a far better place for most with that.

Peace on earth for us all would be a wonderful thing. I hope we can have it one day and I believe we can because if anything is possible, then why not world peace? We don't have to give up on trying to make it so just because someone says it's unrealistic. They said that about aeroplanes once, and I can't tell you how many people said Ian and I couldn't make All On The Board get to 100 followers, or write a bestselling book. Let's give peace a chance.

WRITE WITHOUT FEAR

For better or worse,
anybody can write
lines and a verse;
Words are not a waste of time
if your poem doesn't rhyme;
It can be a quick limerick,
a song or a witty ditty,
Possibly couplets of love
or a hard-hitting sonnet,
Getting down to the nitty gritty.
Everybody has the right to write,
It's quite alright.
An idea can pop up like toast
or appear like the stars at night;
Poems are suitable for all
and can be written by every age;
Set your imagination free from a cage
and let it dance upon the page.
A stutter or a stammer won't affect your grammar,
It doesn't matter if you can't spell;
Every one of us has a novel in us
and potentially a story to tell.
You don't need to have the flows of Jay-Z
or the prose of William Shakespeare;
Just let the sounds of the syllables get stressed
and delightfully write without fear.
If you write down your thoughts today
Will they be similar to those that you write
this time next year?

YOU'RE NOT
A STEPPING STONE

HOW DARE ANYBODY TRY TO TREAT YOU LIKE A
STEPPING STONE;
YOU'RE NOT A RUNNERS-UP MEDAL
OR A SECOND OPTION TO STOP SOMEONE FROM BEING ALONE.
YOUR KINDNESS ISN'T A WEAKNESS, IT'S YOU BEING STRONG,
YOU SHOULDN'T BE TAKEN FOR GRANTED OR
TAKEN ADVANTAGE OF,
YOU ARE WORTH MUCH MORE THAN THAT;
THERE'S ONLY SO MANY TIMES YOU CAN FALL AND BE FOOLED,
YOUR HEART MAY BE OPEN, BUT IT SHOULDN'T ALWAYS BE OPEN
FOR CONTINUOUS HEARTBREAK,
YOU ARE NOT A TWENTY-FOUR-HOUR PETROL STATION,
A BED-AND-BREAKFAST BY THE SEA WITH VACANCIES FOR
MISERY OR A 'WELCOME' DOOR MAT.
AT SOME POINT YOU MAY HEAR THAT OLD CHESTNUT OF,
'IT'S NOT YOU, IT'S ME',
YOU DON'T REALLY NEED REMINDING, IT'S QUITE PLAIN TO SEE;
YOU ARE ENOUGH AND YOUR LOVE SHOULDN'T BE WASTED
ON SOMEONE WITH NO COMMITMENT OR HONESTY.

I'm Not A Medical Expert

I'm not a medical expert with a certificate or a PhD,
All I know is nobody knows me better than me.
Where I am right now in my head I don't want to be;
I'm consumed by jealousy
as positivity plays outside my window
and even from a room with a view I struggle to see.
I complain that my brain is the weakest link in a chain,
It's holding me back and won't set me free;
My mind can be kind sometimes and can truly hold the key,
In the meantime I deserve to get better with
some therapy.
It takes guts when I lose my nerve;
My heart is in the right place
and I should get what I deserve,
But, when I get those butterflies in my stomach,
it takes my breath away;
I want to be well organised from my head to my toes,
But my muscles don't get as much exercise as
my running nose,
Medically speaking, I suppose sometimes it's a positive
to test negative every day.

LIFE
DOESN'T HAVE TO BE
PERFECT
TO BE
BEAUTIFUL

LIFE HAS A WAY OF MAKING YOU FORGET HOW GOOD YOU ARE
AND WHAT YOU'RE LIVING FOR;
THIS IS A LITTLE MESSAGE TO REMIND YOU
THAT YOU ARE EVERYTHING AND SO MUCH MORE.

LIFE IS A JOURNEY
AND LOW SELF-ESTEEM MAY KEEP THE HANDBRAKE ON
AS YOU DRIVE;
DON'T WAIT FOR THE WORLD TO COME TO YOU
LET THE WORLD WAIT FOR YOU TO ARRIVE.

EVERY CHALLENGE IN LIFE WILL HOPEFULLY HELP YOU TO GROW
UNTIL YOU'RE ABLE TO GIVE IT YOUR ALL;
YOU NEED TO FORGIVE YOURSELF
FOR EVERY MISTAKE THAT YOU MAKE,
LIFE DOESN'T HAVE TO BE PERFECT TO BE BEAUTIFUL.

IN NEED
OF REPAIR

IF YOUR CAR WON'T START,
OR IT NEEDS A NEW PART,
YOU WOULD TAKE IT FOR A REPAIR;
DON'T LET IT GO UNSPOKEN,
IF YOU'RE FEELING BROKEN,
THERE ARE PEOPLE THAT GENUINELY CARE.

IF YOUR WASHING MACHINE BROKE,
YOU WOULD CALL OUT A PLUMBER,
YOU WOULDN'T TRY TO FIX IT YOURSELF;
THERE ARE ORGANISATIONS AND
PEOPLE YOU CAN CALL,
TO HELP FIX YOUR MENTAL HEALTH.

POST-TRAUMATIC STRESS DISORDER

IT'S HARD TO BE UPBEAT AND FEEL POSITIVE,
WHEN YOU FEEL YOU HAVE NOTHING LEFT TO GIVE,
AND EVERYDAY YOU SEEM TO LIVE WITH PERSISTENT FEAR,
HORROR, ANGER OR SHAME;
CONSTANT REMINDERS OF AN ATTACK SNEAK UP FROM BEHIND
AND REPLAY FLASHBACKS,
CAUSING DEPRESSION, HALLUCINATIONS, ANXIETY AND DISTORTED BLAME;
SOMETIMES AVOIDING PEOPLE AND PLACES, ACTIVITIES AND SITUATIONS,
CAN LEAVE YOU FRUSTRATED IN ISOLATION WITH POOR CONCENTRATION,
THERE ARE SO MANY TRIGGERS THAT CAN MAKE YOU
RELIVE THE EVENTS IN YOUR MIND;
YOU DON'T HAVE TO BE A SOLDIER OR A VICTIM OF CRIME,
YOU MAY HAVE JUST BEEN IN THE WRONG PLACE AT THE WRONG TIME,
IF YOU'RE TRAUMATISED AND TWISTED BY SURVIVOR GUILT
FROM THE MEMORIES BUILT, YOU NEED HELP TO UNWIND.
INSOMNIA, HYPERVIGILANCE OR A NIGHTMARE REPLACES EACH DREAM,
FEELING HOPELESS AND HELPLESS WITH NEGATIVITY AND
LOW SELF-ESTEEM,
FRIGHTENED AND FIGHTING A LONELY BATTLE IN A PRIVATE WARZONE;
IT'S IMPORTANT TO KNOW IT'S NOT YOUR FAULT,
IF YOU NEED TO TALK OR BE GIVEN DIRECTIONS
FOR THE RIGHT PATH TO WALK,
THERE IS HELP OUT THERE, PLEASE KNOW YOU'RE NOT ALONE.

NIGHT
NOURISHMENTS

Settle down and settle on an
affirmation from this section,

When it's repeated may the selection
give you confidence or bring you
comfort in your head;

May your dreams and wishes come
true with whatever you choose to do,

And may you have a lovely sleep and
pleasant dreams if you're getting
ready for bed.

In reality your fear is small, but it casts a large shadow when you're facing the wall.

To find peace of mind you might have to leave pieces of your life behind.

Do what you need to do to help with your healing, nobody knows how bad you are feeling.

We all get our hearts broken, we all have to grieve, we have moments when we lose faith in ourselves and struggle to believe.

Even a social butterfly can stutter and get flustered as they flutter by.

When you feel like you can't manage, get help or walk away from anyone or anything doing you damage.

You are not weak; you are tired from being strong.

Responsibilities may cause you anxieties, but you can rise above them all.

If you ever believe you're somebody's back up plan, you need to back up and leave as fast as you can.

Mental health is a priority, happiness is essential, and self-care is a necessity.

Respect yourself enough to walk away from a bad situation, you are too special to have your confidence trampled on by abuse and humiliation.

Wounds can be turned into warnings or words of wisdom and truly heard by somebody who really needs them.

You don't need to be rich and famous to be a success, celebrate the achievement of carrying on when you've been going through tough times and dealing with stress.

If you take time out for a minute, you will see that the world hasn't gone wrong, it's just some of the people in it. Keep being you and making the world a better place. You can't control what others do.

A previous love may have turned every promise into dust, but it doesn't mean a promise from somebody else should be one that you can't trust.

Get back up, take a step if you can, then put one foot in front of the other; if you do this enough times you will be heading for a place where you can recover.

True friends will always be there for you, they will stand by your side and cheer you on with pride.

Your demons sometimes knock you down, but they won't get the better of you.

You can rise up and wise up after every defeat.

You don't need to disappear or hide your head in the sand, you just need somebody to listen to you, even if they can't fully understand.

Take more photos and videos of those you love and adore, you never know when they won't be here anymore.

Times have been tough and you've been having it rough, but you will survive because you're strong enough.

Believe in yourself if you believe you're different, because being different means that you're unique; it's much better to stand out rather than being too good at playing hide and seek.

At times it's fine to stop and rewind instead of living life in fast forward.

When you wear your heart on the sleeve of your shirt it doesn't mean you're advertising that you want to be hurt.

Stop doing what you're doing and don't waste another minute, if you're doing it for the wrong reasons and your heart isn't in it.

If you share your feelings with people when you're not feeling great, some things that you say might resonate.

If you're on red alert and your engine is revved up, but you're stuck in a traffic jam, try to educate your mind to just not give a damn.

Sticks and stones may break bones, but words can sometimes kill; if you think 'will this offend someone?', it's highly likely that it will.

Decluttering rooms and tidying up your mind can help to lighten your mood; enrich your life by trying something new like learning another language to cooking exotic food.

At the End of the Day

You are special. You may not feel like it sometimes, but you most certainly are.

No two days are the same, just like no two people are the same, even though days and people share similarities. Some days everything may seem to be going wrong and you may feel like the world and the universe has it in for you, but it honestly hasn't.

Plus, at the end of the day there will always be the start of another. Whatever has happened today is now in the past. Whether it felt like a good experience or bad one, or somewhere in-between, you have got to this point and tomorrow will be a brand new experience. Some days can feel unremarkable and others you just do not want to end, but time and the universe have a way of doing things as they must be done and that can bring everything from grief to happiness your way.

It's important for us to be here for the moments that are meant for us. We are lucky to be alive during a time where so much is possible. We must never lose hope – even when making the most of the day we have in front of us seems impossible – and we must not regret those days that we didn't manage to take hold of. Every day is a gift whatever shape it comes in. Now some days can feel like being given socks for your birthday, in that you may want to give them back, but at the very least they fit. You may have forgotten just how much you need new socks.

If you need help don't be afraid or embarrassed to speak and reach out for help. We all need help sometimes. Even people who appear to have it all figured out, they honestly don't. Some people are just better at hiding things than others, but why should anyone hide anything at all?

You may not know where to go for help or what kind of help you need but, honestly, there is help out there for you with whatever you're going through. Social media and the internet can be a wonderful thing and there are people out there who will give you advice, words of empathy and information that can get you better and feel less alone. Remember: you are not alone. Even if you live on your own or you haven't got any friends or family to turn to. Millions and millions of people are feeling the same way and if we connect with one another and be honest that's when connections are made.

If you are reading this at the end of today, remember you can read it again in a whole new way tomorrow because at the end of the day is a new tomorrow.

Ian and Jeremy x

IAN – A THANK YOU

Thank you to my beautiful wife Salene 'Candis Tonks' Redpath for being so easy to love, for loving me, for being my inspiration, for helping to keep me alive and for being my reason to live. You will forever be my Lady Scoffalot and you know I miss you so much when you're not here. Thanks for also helping to write 'There are many different kinds of love' and 'My Invisible Enemy (well, well, well)' in this book. You are the best thing that's ever happened to me.

Thank you to Brenda Redpath and Terence Redpath (also known as Mum and Dad) for giving me life, showing me love and always being there. I will never be too old to ever hold your hands and it's an absolute pleasure being the son of (possibly) the greatest karaoke singer in the UK and his dancing Queen. Thank you to Nicola Carpenter for being the best big/little sister that a dopey brother could ever ask or wish for. Thank you to my wonderful nephews and nieces Reiss Tonks, Ben Carpenter, Ellie Carpenter (got your full name in this book you absolute diva. Just joking), Susie Waite and Kason Dennard for being amazing and making me feel like a cool uncle when in actual fact I'm an uncool uncle. Although I'm a pretty good dancer when I'm in the mood. Thank you to my Nans and Grandads in Heaven, Nell Ambrose, Ted Ambrose (a fantastic poet and you deserved to have your own poetry books published. Hope you're proud), Walter Redpath and Edith Redpath. Love you loads and see you up there one day.

Thank you to Pip Ambrose, Jay Carpenter (all those late night FIFA sessions on the PlayStation), Sasha Tonks, Natalie Waite, Susan May Tonks (my mother-in-law in Heaven), Pepe the Dog, Marley the Rabbit, Candy the Dog, Charlie the Guinea Pig and all of my family, friends and pets on Earth and in Heaven. You know who you are. I genuinely love you all.

Thank you to these marvellous magicians; Lauren Whelan, Kate Craigie, Liv Nightingall, Jo Myler, Jordan Andrew Carter, Abi Hartshorne, Katy Aries, Jenny Platt and Millie Hoskins for being amazing, helping to put book two together and for putting up with Jeremy and me. And last, but not least . . . Thanks for being YOU!

JEREMY – A THANK YOU

Thank you Kasia for always being there, for reminding me who I am when I'm obsessed or lost in creating, for keeping me alive by making sure I eat when I'm too busy to realise. For your endless love and support, for being the most gorgeous thing I've ever seen, the best mother our wonderful children could ever possibly hope for and quite simply for being the love of my life. I love you more than any book could ever express and I'm incredibly lucky to have you.

Thank you Luna for being your magical dramatic self, a creative creature who far exceeds anything I ever achieved at your age. Never stop believing in yourself and your ideas because you are full of them. You ignite my passion for art every time I think of you. You are full of magic and with a heart like yours there's nothing you cannot do. I love you forever. Thank you Liam for being the coolest, most likeable person in any room. For being the loudest, most energetic and most fun. You remind me of all the coolest kids I never was but always wanted to be. Never lose your spark. It is like no other. I think of you whenever I am trying to be brave. You're my confidence hero and I love you forever too.

Thank you Lizzie, my cat in heaven. I miss your purr and talking meows. Thank you Luli our first family dog. You have brought us all so much love. Thank you Rose and Robbie (my Mum and Dad) for everything you have ever done for me. To all my family, uncles and aunts, friends and all those no longer with us, thank you for being a part of this in ways only the universe can ever express.

Thank you to the amazing team at Yellow Kite who created this book with us. You all smashed it. Lauren Whelan, Kate Craigie, Liv Nightingall, Jo Myler, Jordan Andrew Carter, Abi Hartshorne, Katy Aries and Jenny Platt. What a special book we have made together. Thank you Millie Hoskins for being the best agent in the world.

Thank you to every person who has ever reached out to say thank you, well done or offered messages of support. We appreciate every one of you and hope you know that. May this book bring you as much joy as making it brought us.

First published in Great Britain in 2022 by Yellow Kite
An Imprint of Hodder & Stoughton
An Hachette UK company

1

Cover illustration and chapter openers by Jordan Andrew Carter

A CIP catalogue record for this title is available from the British Library

Hardback ISBN 978 1 399 70520 2

Ebook ISBN 978 1 399 70521 9

Typeset in Gill Sans

Printed and bound in Italy by Elcograf SpA

Hodder & Stoughton policy is to use papers that are natural, renewable and recyclable products and made from wood grown in sustainable forests. The logging and manufacturing processes are expected to conform to the environmental regulations of the country of origin.

Yellow Kite
Hodder & Stoughton Ltd
Carmelite House
50 Victoria Embankment
London EC4Y 0DZ

www.yellowkitebooks.co.uk